Separation of Powers
in the
American Political
System

GEORGE MASON
Painted in 1811 by D. W. Boudet, after a lost portrait by John Hes-
selius.
(Courtesy of the Virginia Museum, Richmond.)

THE GEORGE MASON LECTURES

Separation of Powers in The American Political System

EDITED BY

BARBARA B. KNIGHT

GEORGE MASON UNIVERSITY PRESS
Fairfax, Virginia

Copyright © 1989 by

George Mason University Press

4400 University Drive
Fairfax, VA 22030

All rights reserved

Printed in the United States of America

British Cataloging in Publication Information Available

Distributed by arrangement with
University Publishing Associates, Inc.

4720 Boston Way
Lanham, MD 20706

3 Henrietta Street
London WC2E 8LU England

Library of Congress Cataloging-in-Publication Data

Separation of powers in the American political system /
edited by Barbara B. Knight.
p.   cm. — (The George Mason lectures)
Includes bibliographies.
1. Separation of powers—United States.   I. Knight, Barbara B.
II. Series.
JK305.S48   1989   320.4'04'0973—dc20   89–11760 CIP AC

ISBN 0–913969–26–5 (alk. paper)

All George Mason University Press books are produced on acid-free
paper which exceeds the minimum standards set by the National
Historical Publications and Records Commission.

Contents

Introduction

by

Barbara B. Knight
Associate Professor of Government
George Mason University

Separation of powers is considered one of the most fundamental and unique of the American constitutional principles and at the same time seems to be one of the most misunderstood. Debate continues concerning the original nature and intent of this framework and whether or not the separation of powers as it currently exists in the United States government remains true to the original intent. Two persistent questions are: what is the relationship, if any, of American separation of powers to the older concept of mixed government and what is the connection between the governmental organization of separated powers and the political goal of checks and balances? Underlying both these questions is the basic issue of how the constitutional framers thought limited government and protection of liberty could best be achieved.

This introductory essay will approach these questions by examining important aspects of the theoretical and normative assumptions of the concept of separation of powers. The four essays which follow analyze contemporary separation of powers in the American political system from the perspective of the historical separation and of the place of each of the three branches of government, legislative, executive and judicial, within the overall framework.

In order to understand separation of powers as a means to limit government, particularly in its relation to mixed government and checks and balances, it is useful to begin by comparing and contrasting the conceptual models and normative assumptions from which they are derived.

The Early Development of the Concept of Mixed Government

The theory of mixed government seeks to allocate political authority on the basis of social classes, mixing within one government several types of government. Whatever form the mixture takes, all versions of the mixed regime have intended to create a balance to

1

provide for political stability and to protect against abuses of governmental authority. Institutions, social classes and principles believed to be inherent within these classes were combined in the hope of achieving a judicious balance. Central to the balancing was the provision for law to prescribe the relationship of the classes within the constitutional structure and the role of each class within the governing process.

In contrast to the more modern concept of separation of powers, mixed government derives from classical Greek, Roman and medieval thought. In an early version, the mixture proposed in Plato's *Laws* combined monarchy and democracy. Aristotle presented the mixed regime, or polity, in the *Politics* as a solution to the problem of discovering the best practicable form of government. He sought to discover a regime in which justice could most fully be obtained, one in which the "good man" could also be a "good citizen" because of a coincidence of qualities that were both ethically and politically appropriate. In addition, he believed that this mixed regime would not deteriorate into a perverted form of government, since it was the pure form of government which eventually became perverted.

Aristotle claimed to have discovered a way for citizens to rule in the interest of all: a combination, or mixture, of two classes, oligarchs and democrats, the few rich and the many poor but free. Both classes and principles on which legitimate claims to rule are based, wealth and numbers, were thus combined within one government. A goal was to achieve political stability, halting the cycles of political decay. Power to govern was thus mixed, not divided, in this model.[1]

As Martin Diamond has pointed out, Aristotle believed that in this regime each class contained such radically different human elements from those in other classes that for stability the political system had to include their basic diversity. According to this arrangement each class possessed complete governing power. Each acted as if it alone had final political decision-making power and so could absolutely veto the other element. Hence, in mixed government there is no "give and take" of checks and balances in the way that this arrangement works within a separation of powers framework. In addition, each class was believed to contribute its particular and partial idea of justice to the benefit of the whole community.[2]

While Aristotle wrote of "functions" of government in the *Politics*, he did not conceive of these in terms of legislative, executive and judicial, the contemporary familiar trio. Instead, he described "deliberative" functions, those performed by magistrates, and those by judges. Nor were these functions parcelled out to distinct branches of government; magistrates and the assembly might share deliberative functions, for example.

In the Greek historian Polybius' presentation of a mixed regime the tripartite combination clearly appears. Confronting what he perceived to be the natural cycle of constitutions, from kingship to tyranny, from aristocracy to oligarchy and from democracy to mob rule, Polybius proposed a solution based upon the Spartan model. The only way out of the vicious natural cycle of constitutional deterioration was to adopt a mixed regime combining monarchy, aristocracy and democracy.

It has been suggested that Polybius was the first to combine the concept of the mixed constitution, initially developed by Plato and Aristotle, with a division of power, new with his theory. Aristotle had combined oligarchy and democracy, two forms of government, by concentrating political power in the middle class. This was the group within the society which was believed to be the most moderate. Its members were neither very rich nor very poor and therefore could be counted on to enact only moderate measures. An aim of this regime was to achieve moderation within the government. Here, Aristotle believed, the good man could also be the good citizen.

Polybius' mixture, as he attempted to diagnose the strength of Rome, consisted of elements of monarchy, aristocracy and democracy. Each was to share in the power of the state as each was connected to a particular institution of government. Monarchy was linked to the consulate, aristocracy to the senate, and democracy to the assembly.[3] It is instructive to note the importance of the division of "legislative power" into two parts, senate and assembly, here, since this early "bicameral" mixture points the way to the central role of the two-house legislature in the work of the eighteenth century Frenchman Montesquieu to achieve balanced government.

Cicero also discussed mixed government, analyzing the recently collapsed Roman Republic. His somewhat confusing treatment of material borrowed from Polybius, Plato and Aristotle is not easy to sort out. But he did indicate the importance of population mixture, something about which Polybius was less clear because he had concentrated principally on the formal institutional arrangements. Cicero derived from Polybius the view that a mixed constitution makes it possible to avoid the evils often associated with the pure, or simple, form of government. In his mixed regime, power was dispersed, preventing dangerous concentration, and checks and balances derived from the presence of the several forms of constitution within one government. In language that places him close to Aristotle's concept of mixture, Cicero wrote, "...as in music, harmony is produced by the proportionate blending of unlike tones, so is a state made harmonious by agreement between dissimilar elements brought about by a fair and reasonable blending of the upper, middle and lower classes just as if they were musical tones."[4]

After this, the concept of mixed government went into something of a decline until the time of Thomas Aquinas. As Aquinas retrieved Aristotle's political philosophy, he considered the mixed regime.

Although he favored monarchy under ideal conditions, he found that the stability afforded by a combination of monarchy, aristocracy and democracy provided valuable tempering for a stable regime.

Mixed Government in Eclipse

In the later Middle Ages and Renaissance times, mixed government was referred to only in passing, except in Machiavelli's writings. Although in the *Prince* he advocated a powerful monarch to lead the state to unification, he cited favorably the Spartan and Roman examples of mixed regimes in the *Discourses*. In this, he wrote his commentary on the works of the Roman historian Titus Livy, who himself had drawn on Polybius' works. Machiavelli found classical Sparta and its founding legislator, Lycurgus, praiseworthy for having combined three powers into one government. He believed that this had been done in such a way that stability, endurance and tranquility developed. The prince, nobles and the people brought the elements of the one, the few and the many into one mixed republic. This republican mixed regime was best suited for the long run, in Machiavelli's view; the rule by one man that he advocated in the *Prince* was appropriate for only the founding stage or for weathering severe political crisis.

Dante Germino has pointed to the new facets of Machiavelli's treatment of the mixed state, features which are apparent later in James Madison's analysis of separated powers in the American system. Machiavelli advocated democratic elements in his mixture, and he defended the conflict and competition of opposing interests within the society. The organic class mixture and counterbalancing seem to take second place to this democratic reliance upon the "ordinary" citizens' political competence. His understanding of who qualifies as the citizenry is relatively narrow, and he clearly distinguished mob rule from the recommended popular government. Nevertheless, in this respect, Machiavelli pointed the way toward political competitiveness as a source of governmental strength and foretold liberal democratic elements of popular government.[5]

Underlying these discussions of mixed regimes from ancient to Renaissance times and the theoretical concepts of mixture, balance, moderation and justice contained in them are the values of stability and permanence. Most Greek philosophers had sought to discover the essential "stuff" of which the universe is made. These early speculators were searching for something permanent that could persist through the apparent flux, decay and continual change they perceived to exist in the material world. Their quest for stability and order undergirding apparent confusion and change led some thinkers to posit a single substance underlying the diversity, others to picture the world as a harmonious blend of opposites.[6] This was the same general type of search which characterized the efforts of philosophers to discover some means for achieving stability and permanence in order to thwart the seemingly inexorable forces of political decay and deterioration within the state.

Concern with cycles of governmental growth and decay is inherent in the metaphor of the state as biological organism. The predominant imagery of biological growth and decay in the analogy of state as organism contained the belief that "...the parts had a prescribed, constitutional relationship and combined to make a clearly definable whole."[7] It followed then that many thinkers came to believe that the processes of change endemic to the "organic" state could be halted only by a combination of the basic elements, classes, from each type of state into one mixed constitution. The concept of the mixed regime thus appears to be closely linked to the view of the state as fundamentally organic in its nature.

The dominant sets of ideas which pervade the thought of a particular period in history largely shape the nature of the intellectual models upon which people pattern their thinking. These ideas then stimulate the development of conceptual blueprints, and the thought patterns based on them in turn frequently influence greatly the actual content of the contemporary theoretical speculation. At times it seems as if significant advances or changes in the development of political theory, for example, have come about after scientific discoveries were made which crucially altered the images and models on which all thinking is based.[8]

In the Middle Ages an important image was that of a neat and unchanging hierarchical order that encompassed the entire universe. This permanently fixed order, sometimes described as a "great chain of being," ran all the way from God at the top to the lowest form of matter at the bottom. "Here was the teleological hierarchy of the Aristotelian forms, all heading up in God or Pure Form, with man intermediate in reality and importance between him and the material world."[9] This was combined with a view of the universe as existing solely for man, with man at the center in every sense. Nature was thought to exist for the sake of man and also, therefore, to be immediately and fully intelligible to his reason.[10] A similar paradigm of right order was frequently proposed for a single state as well, with a king at the top and the classes arranged down the hierarchy according to the immutable divine plan. Various theories of monarchical rule, including the divine right of kings, were fostered by this world view. Indeed, such a world view makes highly unlikely any call for a marked diminution or sharing of power in the position at the apex of the natural order. It was Dante's vision in the *Divine Comedy* that led to his proposal for a world monarch, one ruler over all earth, modelled on the order of the monotheistic hierarchical universe. In the face of this world view, theories of mixed government tended to recede somewhat in importance.

The Mechanical Concept of Balanced Government

The work of scientists such as Copernicus, Kepler, and Tycho Brahe shattered the geocentric and essentially simple Ptolemaic pattern of the universe on which the "great chain of being" was based. Their discoveries concerning the earth's motion and mathematics of astronomy led Galileo to wonder if the motions of small parts of the earth's crust might not also be mathematically reducible. He built upon Descartes' earlier conviction that mathematics held the key to the secrets of the natural world, and he eventually concluded that the "real" world is indeed mathematical. In England, empirical scientific movements were developing, guided by such men as Gilbert, Harvey and Robert Boyle. Harvey's studies of the circulation of blood through the body led to a view of human beings as mechanical objects. The chemist Boyle's almost religious zeal resulted in his attempts to combine a view of God as divine providence with the concept of the world as an immense clock-like machine which God originally set into motion and which subsequently runs on its own.[11]

The way was thus paved for the scientific outlook of Isaac Newton. Newtonian physics represented the apex of a mechanical interpretation of the world. Descartes had spoken of God as maintaining the vast machine of the universe; Boyle frequently compared the world to the Strassburg clock. Newton conceived of God as the chief mechanic of the universe, the cosmic conservative, working to preserve the perfect status quo.[12] Newton's notion of balance influenced the changes in normative assumptions which led to the shift from mixed government to separation of powers as an organizing governmental principle. For Newton, the entire universe could be conceptualized as a gigantic clock with all its elements, including the political state, in similar balance.

Karl Deutsch discussed the importance of the shift in dominant imagery from the earlier and simpler biological images to the more recent mechanistic models. He has pointed out that only after complex mechanical operations developed toward the end of the Middle Ages could mechanical models of greater complexity than were previously known emerge. Most significantly, mechanisms had the unique capacity of being able to be taken apart and then reassembled exactly as they were before. In addition, the

> ...development of clockwork...yielded the classic model of a
> 'mechanism'—a model applied to a description of the stars in
> the system of Newton; to government in the writings of
> Machiavelli and Hobbes; 'checks and balances' by Locke,
> Montesquieu, and the founding fathers of the American
> Constitution....[13]

Classic mechanism also

...implied the notion of a whole that was completely equal to the sum of its parts, that could be run in reverse, and that would behave in exactly identical fashion no matter how often those parts were dis-assembled and put together again....It thus implied the notion that the parts were never significantly modified by each other....

As this model implied certain assumptions, so it excluded others. The notions of irreversible change, of growth, of evolution, of novelty, and of purpose all had no place in it.[14]

When it is based upon the mechanistic model, the state eventually becomes conceived of as an instrument created for specific functions, much like a machine. The analogy differs from the earlier organic images in that they inevitably presumed a more inclusive, essentially unorganized substratum for the state to rest on. The newer concept of the state is not considered to be inclusive of all activities of the persons within the political association.[15] As this new model persisted, the scope for the political realm narrowed, eventually resulting in the concept of "negative government."

In the early half of the seventeenth century, however, differences of outlook produced varying reactions to the "right" organization of political power. Thomas Hobbes and John Milton responded to the political events of the mid 1600s in England and evaluated the mixed regime as a possible prescription for resolving the political crisis. Interpreting the crisis as one of political authority, Hobbes sought a solution that would result in a restoration of authority sufficient to maintain peace and order in the wake of continuing and deep civil unrest. He rejected the mixed constitution as the solution on at least two grounds: first, it could result in a restriction on liberty as much as could a simple form of government if the three branches of government which constituted the mixture were to act in concert. Second, if there were conflict and checking among the various powers, the theoretical advantage of the division would be achieved but, for Hobbes, this would be at the expense of crippling authority and the end result would be once again civil war and governmental collapse. Hobbes viewed sovereignty in the way Bodin had earlier, as either indivisible or essentially non-existent.[16] Much of what Hobbes advocated for the political institutions in a government with sufficient authority to survive was based in his pessimistic view of human nature, as essentially warring, brutish and nasty. Strong coercive political authority was deemed necessary to hold society in place.

On the other hand, John Milton favorably compared the Puritan Commonwealth to the system praised by Polybius as responsible for the power and grandeur of Rome. Milton attributed much of the excellence of the English government to its mixed character. Neither monarchy, aristocracy nor democracy, it was instead a mixture retaining the claims of each, Milton judged. The balance, he believed, was harmoniously tuned, with a mixture and temperament including the virtues of each of the other forms of state.

The "free Commonwealth" he advocated when he rejected all monarchies, even constitutional ones after the events of the 1640s in England, had elements of Polybius' mixed constitution, he thought: magistracy or monarchy embodied in the Council of State, aristocracy in the Grand Council, or legislature, and democracy in the electoral process for local offices and for the Grand Council members. Such an arrangement of the Commonwealth was aimed at achieving balance within the government.

As Walter Berns has discerned after his analysis of the institutional features involved in Milton's model, the balance envisioned is not achieved by setting class against class in an institutional opposition. Milton's constitutional government was instead a mixture of aristocracy (or oligarchy) and democracy, achieved by the rule of what he termed the "middle sort." He thought this was the "true aristocracy," or "rule by the best." For Milton, these best men were distinguished by their character and by public service.[17] Milton's view of the "middle sort" of men as noble, prudent and worthy is a far cry from Thomas Hobbes' view of natural man.

In some ways, Milton's mixed regime seems to resemble that of Aristotle more than any other classical thinker's. Yet he departs from even Aristotle, since Christian liberty is for Milton the ultimate purpose of life and, of course, of political rule. The Commonwealth has as its purpose something that lies beyond it, transcends it, and so the political realm shrinks somewhat in scope and in value.

Contributions of Locke and Montesquieu

The concepts of checking and balancing which developed at this time played an important role in the England of Cromwell and later. It was here that the outbreak of hostilities between the King and Parliament prompted attempts to redefine the relative functions of these elements of the government and the means whereby each might be balanced and held in check by the other, in order to prevent tyranny from any quarter.

Carl Friedrich has pointed to Cromwell's *Instrument of Government*, issued in 1653, as a first attempt to distinguish and separate executive and legislative power.[18] It has been suggested that it was at this general period in history that the theory of separation of powers began to develop, replacing that of mixed government, when the latter proved inadequate to institutionalize the emerging political values.

By the year of the execution of Charles I...the doctrine of the separation of powers, in one form or another, had emerged in England, but as yet it was still closely related to the theory of mixed government. It had been born of the latter theory but had not yet torn itself away to live an independent life....The execution of king, and the abolition of the House of Lords, destroyed the institutional basis of the theory of mixed government and any justification of the new constitution which was to be framed for England would have to rest on a different theoretical basis.[19]

Changes that came about in seventeenth century England, philosophically and politically, altered the concept of mixed government even as it was being increasingly employed by political theorists. Gabriel Almond has pointed out that classical political theory stressed the connections of social classes with political classification and political change. The internal operations of the political processes were not dealt with in any depth. On the other hand, the seventeenth and eighteenth century political theorists in Britain focused directly on the political system itself and placed emphasis on the internal separation of functions and powers. Thus, Almond saw the emergence of a specifically political theory of separation of powers and checks and balances.[20]

In the second half of the seventeenth century, and specifically after 1660, the doctrine of separated powers went into temporary eclipse in England. Scholars differ about why this happened, but the most useful explanation seems to be acceptance of mixed monarchy as the best form of government. The fact that separated powers was associated with "republicanism" may have abetted this tendency.[21] What has occasioned even more debate is whether or not any important theory of separation of powers can be found in the work of John Locke. In contrast to such Lockean scholars as Peter Laslett and Ernest Barker, William Gwyn posits the connection of Locke with separation of powers as part of his version of the rule of law. For Locke, one of the essential conditions for enjoying increased security and civil liberty under government was the separation of legislative from executive functions. It seems that Locke believed that without this crucial separation, liberty would be less secure even than it had been in the state of nature. Certainly Locke's view of separation of powers, however entangled it may still be with mixed government, provides a significant theoretical bridge to the ideas of Montesquieu and eventually to those of the American Founding Fathers.[22]

Locke's division of governmental power into legislative, executive and federative resulted in combining executive and judicial power and separating out foreign or external affairs. His concern seemed to be primarily with the division between legislative and executive power since he feared that it would give too much control to those who make laws to carry them out as well.

A key to understanding the differences between mixed government and separation of powers is the realization that mixed government presupposes a mixed society, with qualitatively differentiated regime elements, and that separation of powers presupposes an individually heterogeneous democracy. Thus, for both Locke and Montesquieu in the eighteenth century, the mixed regime and separation of powers would still be at least somewhat entangled since the political environment contained elements of both organic mixed society and atomistic heterogeneous society. The transition from one to the other was under way, but was not yet complete.[23]

Montesquieu's principal concern was with discovering a constitutional principle on which moderate governments could be developed, since moderate government was in his view the way to insure the maintenance of political liberty. He was clear from the outset that the basic protection against tyranny was to be found in dividing the government into legislative, executive and judicial functions and further to subdivide the legislative function into two bodies. It is here that Montesquieu clearly combines mixed government theory with that of separated powers. In fact, the legislative process itself formed the source of a three-layered mixture. The legislature included the monarch acting in his legislative capacity, the aristocracy and the democratic element. Henry Merry observed that for Montesquieu separation of legislative, executive and judicial functions was principally a take-off point. What political liberty requires in his view is that each of the monarchical, aristocratic and democratic forces be included.[24] The end product for Montesquieu was a version of mixed government closely theoretically related to that of Aristotle and also a proposal for separation of powers which drew from Locke and other English thinkers to point forward to the American doctrines of separation of powers and checks and balances.

The classical theory of mixed government, based on the mixture of classes, was crucial in the overall development of Montesquieu's theory of separation of powers. Fernand Cattelain has pointed out that in Montesquieu's thought one can recognize two distinct, though related, theories which he has fused together: the theory of dividing powers into legislative, executive and judicial and the theory of combining three forms of government, monarchy, aristocracy and democracy.[25] But even more than the combination of forms, Montesquieu envisioned a combination or mixture of the social or class elements which traditionally held the principal political power in each of the three forms of government as the critical focus for his system.

Although Montesquieu separated powers on a functional and institutional basis, the basic foundation on which this division was established remained largely a class division. Each class within the society was ascribed a particular principle or spirit, which served as its special contribution to the political system as a whole. As was the case in the older theories of mixed regime, the spirit attributed to each class was derived from the particular form of government in which that class constituted the dominant element. In Montesquieu's formulation, monarchy was believed to bring to the government the spirit of honor, aristocracy to supply moderation, and democracy to contribute virtue. These were then to be mixed together into one government by their distribution among the governmental functions. The most important point of distribution was that within the legislative function, to two separate bodies in a bicameral arrangement.[26] Montesquieu's version of the mixed regime, combined as it was with a separation of powers scheme, contained the underlying assumption that there could be no liberty where executive, legislative and judicial powers are united in one person or body of persons. Instead, such an arrangement of concentrated power was thought to result in a despotic government.

The Change From Mixed Polity to Separation of Functions

In Montesquieu's writings, separation of powers and balance of powers are presented as two distinct, yet interdependent, principles of liberty. Montesquieu defined political liberty in various ways in the *Spirit of the Laws*. Among the most important of these are two: 1) liberty as the ability to do what one ought to will and the freedom from having to do what one ought not to will, and 2) liberty as the right of doing what the laws permit. The protection of liberty, therefore, was interwoven with the content of the laws and was possible only when those laws resulted from and in turn maintained moderate, balanced government. Implicit in Montesquieu's political theory, as well as for many British thinkers who closely preceded him, was the belief that liberty, understood in this way, could best be obtained in a system characterized primarily by "negative government." Ferdinand Hermens, discussing the thought of Montesquieu, pointed out the critical fact that the term and the concept of "balance" found in Montesquieu's work was derived principally from an analogy to the field of physics. In that discipline, the term balance was most frequently employed in connection with a pair of scales. In order for these scales to be in a condition of "balance," there must necessarily be a complete equality of forces on both sides. The ultimate implication of this is an absence of movement. Hermens stated that: "In the language of the political field this can mean only one thing: a 'deadlock' ...with the potentiality of a stalemate...."[27] He pointed out further that the possible dangers inherent within such a deadlocked system, based as it is on a rigid separation of powers, result not only from this fact, that the "balance" may lead to political deadlock, but that when there is any danger at all that such deadlock might develop, the demand for action will become so strong that any response to it will be accepted out of desperation, even if it sweeps organic checks aside together with the balances.

It has been argued that Montesquieu apparently valued the English constitution above all because of the difficulties which it managed to place in the way of rapid and efficient action. The constitution, and the system of separated powers upon which he believed it to rest, contradicted Richelieu's ideal of rapidity and efficiency in government, exactly what Montesquieu was opposing with his theory. To support this interpretation, A. J. Grant quoted Montesquieu's point that the natural result of the British system would be to establish "repose and inaction; but as by the necessary movement of things they are forced to move, they will be forced to move in harmony."[28]

The logical conclusion of this line of theoretical speculation is the belief that since liberty is best achieved for the individual when there is checking and balancing of governmental functions and of the social and economic groupings, individual freedom is fostered by the resulting governmental deadlock and threatened by political action. Government is conceived of as the embodiment of conflict and opposition of the differing groups and interests rather than as a matter of cooperation and movement in concert.

Because the theory of separation of powers and checks and balances became so closely bound up with the limited government proponents in political thought, its importance in European political thought declined drastically when the extreme versions of "limited" government or "negative" government were left behind. In the main, these were ultimately replaced by the more activist theories of numerical majorities, such as those found in the work of J. S. Mill, and by the "idealism" of political thinkers such as T.H. Green and Bernard Bosanquet. Therefore, for the next stage in the development of the theoretical concept of separation of powers, we must cross the Atlantic to find its adaptation to the American experience by the Founding Fathers as they drafted the U.S. Constitution at the end of the eighteenth century. As Martin Diamond pointed out, while even in the works of Montesquieu the theories of the mixed regime and of separation of powers were still somewhat entangled, in the founding of the American government, separation of powers finally reached its own distinct formulation.[29]

Simple versus Complex Government in America

The American founders were familiar with the concept of the mixed regime. Whatever its form, a mixed regime presupposes that there is a mixed society, with the different regime elements, or groupings, present. Among the statesmen of this period, John Adams is perhaps the one who remained most attached to the mixed form of government. His advocacy of separation of powers seems to include the mixed regime, as if the two were essentially interdependent. Any of his discussion of separated powers was bound up with his desire for some form of mixed government.

Adams stressed the importance and inevitability of the natural inequalities among men. He believed these stemmed from many sources, including differences in wealth, talent and family background. These differences, he felt, were the source of a natural aristocracy which must be carefully managed in order to prevent danger to the political system. Adams believed that the differences are the source of a deep and fundamental cleavage within society, and so government must function to protect the interests of each major class. Each group deserved protection of its unequal status and possessions.

Although anxious to protect the holdings of the aristocratic minority against the majority, Adams was aware of the aristocracy's capacity to abuse power. In his view, government by the many would despoil the holdings of the few, and government by the few would pose danger to the rights of the many poor. The ultimate answer lay in establishing a unit of government to represent each of the two major units of the society. In Adams' model, the chief executive would hold the balance between the two. If he were to threaten to abuse his power, his actions would be checked by the legislature. Thus it was that to support the mixture in the regime Adams proposed something similar to Montesquieu's functional separation of powers. The key to the balance was to be found in the legislative arrangement. Thus Adams would superimpose separation of powers on a mixed regime. His own model for this seems to have been the theory, if not the practice, of the English constitution, as described by Sir William Blackstone in his *Commentaries on the Laws of England*.[30]

In analyzing the positions favored by the Anti-Federalists in the late eighteenth century, Herbert Storing contrasted their views with those of Adams. A key difference turned on the preferred structural nature of the government: simple or complex. Storing found much support among Anti-Federalists for a simple form of government. They emphasized responsibility in government more than balance, and, along with Thomas Paine, tended to view simple government as providing the clearest lines of political accountability. People could easily and quickly spot the source of power abuse, whereas they believed that complex government tends to set up a smoke screen effect, obscuring the location of the fault. The preference of many Anti-Federalists was for simple, responsible government, based in a small and relatively homogeneous population.[31]

As they recognized that the Constitution would not establish a simple form of government, many Anti-Federalists believed that the alternative complex government should be based on the model of a mixed government that stems from fixed orders or divisions within society. The result would be a "real" system of checks and balances, in which the natural orders found in society would be institutionalized within the legislature. Among those who advocated this approach,

Patrick Henry stood out as favoring what he viewed as real checks founded on "self-love," not "paper" checks. Without checks and balances based on the interests of permanent orders, Henry feared that the checks would be only theoretical, "ideal," not real ones. Thus the protection for liberty resulting from checks and balances within the mixed regime would be absent.

Storing concluded that many Anti-Federalists criticized the Constitution because it fell between the two stools of mixed government, with balance deriving from the combination of monarchy, aristocracy and democracy, on the one hand, and simple, clearly responsible government, on the other.[32] It seems that either of these types could be viewed as accomplishing the preservation of liberty as the Anti-Federalists understood it.

Separation of Powers in the American Constitution

The novel aspect of the separation of powers and checks and balances in the American Constitution is its combination with republican popular government and detachment from the old mixture of types of government and classes within one political system.[33] Society and government are clearly distinguished and separated, with an accompanying reduction in the scope of the political and expansion of the private sphere.

Whereas in mixed government, the people were divided (into classes or estates) and the government undivided, in the arrangement of separation of powers the people are undivided (in the European sense of social segmentation) and the governmental power divided and dispersed. Pointing out this difference, James Monroe noted that previously the objective of distributing powers had been intended to preserve a mixture of monarchy, aristocracy and democracy with the goal of maintaining a balance of these elements within the regime. The American separation of powers, however, was designed to prevent unified governmental power.[34]

Separation of powers as developed in the U. S. Constitution depends first on a differentiation of governmental "tasks" or functions. These functions, legislative, executive and judicial, are then distributed to separate and distinct institutions for the sake of efficiency as well as for dividing power. These branches are set up to be independent of each other: no one is dependent upon the other for staying in office and each is constituted and empowered separately by an article of the Constitution.

In part deriving from a particular view of human nature, that men are "not angels," but rather are self-interested individuals, indicated by James Madison in *Federalist* 51, the functionally divided power is then overlapped sufficiently to provide for checking and balancing. This overlap is first a functional one, including such features as the presidential veto of congressional legislation, legislative override of the veto and judicial review. Beyond this, and central to the goal of checking interest with interest, power with power, the constituency for each of the branches of government is different. Because the members of each respond to different mixes of interests, there can result the kind of "self-interest rightly understood" that prevents majority tyranny and enhances liberty.

Separating powers through functional and institutional division and establishing checks and balances based on both constitutional devices, such as the presidential veto, and personal interest connected to office are the result of what Alexander Hamilton referred to in *Federalist* 9 as the "greatly improved science of politics." Ambition can then counteract ambition and the political futures, as well as personal interests of the office holders, will be linked electorally to different mixes of factional interests to which they will be both responsive and accountable.

According to Storing's study, many Anti-Federalists feared that the resulting form of government benefited neither from the virtue of simple government, allowing for clear and easy accountability, nor from the mixed regime's capacity to provide effective internal checks by means of the combination of different orders within society, either those present in Europe or the "natural" orders emerging in American society. Instead of a mixed government, there were now separation of powers and checks and balances, believed by many Anti-Federalists to be insufficient measures to protect liberty.[35]

From the framers' point of view, the separation of powers with checks and balances, now fully detached from mixed government and based in different normative assumptions, was a creative approach to establishing an unmixed form of government. Instead of combining several types of rule into one system, they chose one form, popular government, and developed constitutional arrangements to divide political power within that government. When set into motion in the large, pluralistic American society, the result was intended to be a version of popular government that would combine a workable balance of self interest and public good, of individual liberty and governmental authority. How this original arrangement has evolved over the past two centuries and its current status are the subject of the rest of this book.

Sponsored by the Center for the Study of Constitutional Rights, the lecture series on which this volume was based was made possible by grants from Howard D. Orebaugh, President, United Savings Bank, Vienna, Virginia, and the Graduate School, George Mason University. Among those members of the University who have been most helpful to the project are George Johnson, President; Charles K. Rowley, Dean, the Graduate School; Ruth Kerns, Fenwick Library; and Robert T. Hawkes, Jr., Dean, School of Continuing and Alternative Learning. G. Marvin Tatum of Fenwick Library prepared the index. We are also especially grateful to A. E. Dick Howard, University of Virginia School of Law, for his very helpful work as Chief Consultant since the project's commencement. Finally, my appreciation to two colleagues and friends, Josephine Pacheco and Daniel Shumate, Director and Associate Director respectively of the Center, for giving me the opportunity to be a part of this project and for their help and encouragement throughout.

Barbara B. Knight
George Mason University

Endnotes

1. Martin Diamond, "Separation of Powers and the Mixed Regime," *Publius*, 8 (Summer 1978), 35.
2. Ibid.
3. Walter Berns, "Milton," in Leo Strauss and Joseph Cropsey, *History of Political Philosophy*, 2d ed. (Chicago: Rand McNally, 1972), pp. 416–17.
4. C. G. Richards, *Cicero: A Study* (London: Chatto and Woods, 1935), p. 298.
5. Machiavelli, *The Prince and The Discourses*, ed. Max Lerner (New York: Modern Library, 1940), p. 116 ff. See also Dante Germino, *Machiavelli to Marx: Modern Western Political Thought* (Chicago: University of Chicago Press, 1972), pp. 48–52.
6. Kathleen Freeman, *The Pre-Socratic Philosophers* (Oxford: Basil Blackwell, 1946), pp. 40–50.
7. Thomas Jenkin, *The Study of Political Theory* (New York: Doubleday, 1955), p. 29.
8. See Thomas Kuhn, *The Structure of Scientific Revolutions* 2d ed., (Chicago: University of Chicago, 1978).
9. E.A. Burtt, *The Metaphysical Foundations of Modern Physical Science* (New York: Doubleday, n.d.), p. 98.
10. Ibid., p. 18.
11. Ibid., p. 206.
12. Ibid., p. 292.
13. Karl Deutsch, *Nerves of Government* (New York: Free Press, 1963), p. 26.
14. Ibid., p. 27.
15. Jenkin, pp. 29–30.
16. Laurence Berns, "Thomas Hobbes," in Strauss and Cropsey, pp. 385–86.
17. Walter Berns, pp. 418–29.
18. Carl Friedrich, *Constitutional Government and Democracy* (Boston: Ginn, 1950), pp. 175–76.
19. M.J.C. Vile, *Constitutionalism and the Separation of Powers* (Oxford: Clarendon Press, 1967), p. 40. See also W. B. Gwyn, *The Meaning of Separation of Powers* (New Orleans: Tulane University, 1965), for elaboration of this point.
20. Gabriel Almond, "Political Theory and Political Science," *American Political Science Review*, LX, 4 (December, 1966), p. 871.
21. Gwyn, p. 67.
22. Ibid., Ch. 5.
23. Diamond, p. 40.

24. Henry Merry, *Montesquieu's System of Natural Government* (W. Lafayette, Indiana: Purdue University, 1970), p. 373.
25. Fernand Cattelain, *Etude sur l'influence de Montesquieu dans les constitutions Americaines* (Besancon: Imprimerie Millot Freres, 1927), p. 31.
26. Gwyn, pp. 111–13.
27. Ferdinand A. Hermens, *The Representative Republic* (Notre Dame: University of Notre Dame, 1958), pp. 437–38.
28. A.J. Grant, "Montesquieu," in F.J.C. Hearnshaw, ed. *The Social and Political Ideas of Some Great French Thinkers of the Age of Reason* (London: Dawsons, 1967), p. 128.
29. Diamond, p. 35.
30. Alan P. Grimes, *American Political Thought*, rev. ed. (Lanham, Md.: United Press of America, 1983), pp. 110–13.
31. Herbert Storing, *What the Anti-Federalists Were For* (Chicago: University of Chicago, 1981), pp. 56–60.
32. Ibid., pp. 58–59.
33. See Alexander Hamilton, James Madison and John Jay, *The Federalist*, Jacob E. Cooke, ed. (Middletown, Ct.: Wesleyan University, 1961), especially Numbers 9, 10, 47 and 51.
34. Storing, pp. 61–63.
35. Ibid.

The Allocation of Powers: The Framers' Intent

Louis Fisher
Congressional Research Service, Library of Congress

The "separation of powers" doctrine is considered America's unique contribution to political stability. Yet this doctrine remains a highly elusive concept. In both theory and practice, it teems with subtleties, ironies, and apparent contradictions. Just what the framers intended is a subject of continuing dispute, spawning a vast literature with varying interpretations. Even if we could agree on the "framers' intent," the relationships among the three branches of government have changed fundamentally in two centuries to produce novel arrangements and peculiar overlappings.

The Separation Doctrine

Critics of separated powers in America claim that this system produces intolerable deadlocks and inefficiency, especially for a twentieth-century government expected to exercise worldwide responsibilities. However, there is no necessary link between separated powers and inefficiency. The framers did not adopt a separation of powers to obstruct government. They wanted to create a system in 1787 that would operate more effectively and efficiently than the discredited Articles of Confederation, written in 1777 and ratified in 1781.

Only one branch of national government existed before 1787: the Continental Congress. There was no executive or judiciary. Members of the Congress had to legislate and then serve on committees to administer and adjudicate what they had passed. Within a few years the system proved to be so exhausting, inept, and embarrassing that it became necessary to delegate administrative and judicial duties to outside bodies. To relieve committees of administrative details, Congress turned to boards staffed by people outside the legislature. When these multi-headed boards failed to supply energy and accountability, Congress appointed single executive officers in 1781 to run the executive departments, a Secretary for Foreign Affairs, a Superintendent of Finance, a Secretary at War, and a Secretary of Marine.

These departments supplied a vital link in administrative machinery between the Continental Congress and the national government established in 1787.[1] When John Jay took over as Secretary for Foreign Affairs in 1784, he served throughout the remaining years of the Continental Congress. He even continued in that same capacity as Acting Secretary of State under Washington's first administration, until Thomas Jefferson assumed the duties of Secretary of State in March 1790. Henry Knox was Secretary at War from 1785 until the final days of 1794. Still another example of administrative continuity was Joseph Nourse, who served as Register of the Treasury from 1779 to 1829.[2]

The Continental Congress also established the beginnings of a national judiciary by setting up Courts of Admiralty to decide all controversies over naval captures and the distribution of war prizes. By 1780 Congress had created the Court of Appeals in Cases of Capture, which functioned until its last session on May 16, 1787, at the State House in Philadelphia across the hall from the room in which delegates were assembling for the Constitutional Convention.[3]

This separation of legislative, executive, and judicial functions was determined principally by events and experience, not theory. In a striking phrase, the historian Francis Wharton said that the Constitution "did not make this distribution of power. It would be more proper to say that this distribution of power made the Constitution of the United States."[4] Justice Brandeis spoke a half-truth when he claimed that the doctrine of separated powers was "adopted by the Convention of 1787, not to promote efficiency but to preclude the exercise of arbitrary power."[5] Efficiency was a key objective.[6]

It is often said that powers are separated to preserve liberties. It is equally true that a rigid separation can *destroy* liberties by making government ineffective. The historic swings in France between executive and legislative dominance suggest the danger of extreme separation. The French constitutions of 1791 and 1848, which established a pure separation of powers, ended in absolutism and reaction.[7] The American framers wanted to avoid political fragmentation and paralysis of power. Joseph Story, a distinguished constitutional commentator and member of the Supreme Court, knew that a rigid adherence to separated powers "in all cases would be subversive of the efficiency of the government, and result in the destruction of the public liberties."[8] Justice Jackson described the complex elements that coexist in America's separation doctrine: "While the Constitution diffuses power the better to secure liberty, it also contemplates that the practice will integrate the dispersed powers into a workable government. It enjoins upon its branches separateness but interdependence, autonomy but reciprocity."[9]

Although the separation of powers doctrine is not expressly stated in the Constitution, it is implied in the allocation of legislative powers to the Congress in Article I, executive powers to the President in Article II, and judicial powers to the Supreme Court in Article III. Several provisions help reinforce the separation. Article I, Section 6, prohibits members of either House of Congress from holding any other civil office. This is called the Incompatibility Clause and has been difficult to litigate. In 1974 the Supreme Court denied standing to plaintiffs who challenged the right of members of Congress to hold a commission in the armed forces reserves.[10] The vitality of the Incompatibility Clause is thus left largely to the practices of the executive and legislative branches. This is one of many areas in which the meaning of the Constitution depends not on the Supreme Court but on working relationships and accommodations between the two other branches.

Article I, Section 6, also prohibits members of Congress from being appointed to any federal office created during their term of office, or to any federal position whose salary has been increased during their term of office. This is called the Ineligibility Clause or the Emoluments Clause. The framers were aware that members of the British Parliament had been corrupted by appointments to office from the Crown, but they were also reluctant to exclude qualified and able people from public office.[11]

To reconcile these conflicting goals, Congress has at times reduced the salary of an executive position to permit someone from the House or the Senate to be appointed to the post. For example, after Congress had increased the salary of the Secretary of State from $8,000 to $12,000, President Taft wanted to name Senator Philander Knox to that office in 1909. A special bill was drafted to reduce the compensation of the Secretary of State to the original figure. The bill inspired heated debate in the House of Representatives but was enacted into law.[12] Knox was then nominated by President Taft and confirmed by the Senate. A similar situation arose in 1973 concerning the nomination of Senator William Saxbe as Attorney General after Congress had increased the salary of that office from $35,000 to $60,000. Legislation was enacted to keep Saxbe's compensation at $35,000.[13] The debate offers a good example of the manner in which Congress and the Executive engage in constitutional construction.[14] Although a literal interpretation of the Ineligibility Clause would have eliminated Knox and Saxbe from consideration, legislation was passed to preserve the spirit, if not the letter, of the Clause.

There are other safeguards for the separation doctrine. Congress is prohibited from reducing the compensation of the President and members of the judiciary. As Hamilton noted in *Federalist* 79, an independent judiciary requires a secure salary "a power over a man's subsistence amounts to a power over his will." When Congress disapproved federal pay raises from 1975 to 1979, the Supreme Court held in 1980 that two of the rescissions violated the Constitution because they diminished the salaries of federal judges.[15]

The Speech or Debate Clause provides legislative immunity to protect members of Congress from executive or judicial harassment. The language of Article I, Section 6, reads: "for any Speech or Debate in either House," Senators or Representatives "shall not be questioned in any other Place." The courts have consistently held that the immunities offered by this Clause exist not simply for the personal or private benefit of members "but to protect the integrity of the legislative process by insuring the independence of individual legislators."[16] Article I, Section 6, also provides that members of Congress "shall in all cases, except treason, felony and breach of the peace, be privileged from arrest during their attendance at the session of their respective houses, and in going to and returning from the same." Immunity from arrest during sessions of the legislature can be traced back to struggles between the English Parliament and the King.

Several sections of the Constitution produce combinations, not separations, of the branches. The President may veto legislation, subject to a two-thirds override vote of each House. Some of the Anti-Federalists objected that the veto allowed the President to encroach upon the legislature, but Hamilton in *Federalist* 73 defended the qualified veto on two grounds: it protected the President's office against legislative "depredations," and it served as a check on bad laws.

Presidents also exercise a "pocket veto." Any bill not returned by the President "within ten Days (Sundays excepted)" shall become law "unless the Congress by their Adjournment prevent its Return, in which Case it shall not be a Law." Several decisions have effectively eliminated the use of a pocket veto during a congressional session.[17] The remaining legal issue concerns the President's power to pocket veto a bill between the first and second sessions.[18] There is no question about the President's power to invoke the pocket veto at the end of the second session when a Congress adjourns.

The Constitution contains other overlappings. The President nominates officers but the Senate confirms. He submits treaties for Senate ratification. The House of Representatives may impeach executive and judicial officers, subject to the Senate's conviction in a trial. If the President is impeached, the Chief Justice of the Supreme Court presides during the trial in the Senate. The courts decide convictions but the President may pardon offenders. Under its implied powers, Congress may also participate by passing amnesty statutes and offering witnesses absolute immunity from prosecution if they testify.

These mixtures led to complaints by several delegates at the state ratifying conventions. They objected that the branches of government had been intermingled instead of being kept separate. "How is the executive?," cried one delegate at the Virginia ratifying convention. "Contrary to the opinion of all the best writers, blended with the legislative. We have asked for bread, and they have given us a stone."[19] The Constitution was attacked in the North Carolina and the Pennsylvania ratifying conventions for violating the separation doctrine.[20] These three states insisted that a separation clause be added to the national bill of rights. The language considered by Congress is as follows: "The powers delegated by this constitution are appropriated to the departments to which they are respectively distributed so that the legislative department shall never exercise the powers vested in the executive or judicial [,] nor the executive exercise the powers vested in the legislative or judicial, nor the judicial exercise the powers vested in the legislative or executive departments."[21]

By the time of the Philadelphia convention, the doctrine of separated powers had been overtaken by the system of checks and balances. One contemporary pamphleteer dismissed the separation doctrine, in its pure form, as a "hackneyed principle" and a "trite maxim."[22] Madison devoted several of his *Federalist* essays to the need for overlapping powers, claiming that the concept was superior to the impracticable partitioning of powers demanded by some Anti-Federalists. Hamilton, in *Federalist* 75, defended the combination of the Executive with the Senate in the treaty process and bristled at "the trite topic of the intermixture of powers." The separation clause—proposed by Virginia, North Carolina, and Pennsylvania—was rejected by Congress. Also voted down was a substitute amendment to make the three departments "separate and distinct."[23]

Strict constructionists regard the Constitution as one of enumerated powers. They oppose the notion of implied powers, inherent powers, powers derived from custom, or any other extraconstitutional power not explicitly granted to one of the three branches. While there is legitimate concern about the scope of implied powers, all three branches find it necessary to exercise powers not stated in the Constitution. Congress has the power to investigate as a necessary function of its legislative power; the President has the power to remove certain administrative officials to maintain executive accountability and responsibility; the Supreme Court has acquired the power to review legislative, executive, and state actions on questions of constitutionality.

The framers recognized the need for implied powers. Madison noted in *Federalist* 44: "No axiom is more clearly established in law, or in reason, than that whenever the end is required, the means are authorized; whenever a general power to do a thing is given, every particular power necessary for doing it is included." Congress was granted not merely the enumerated power found within Article I but was also authorized to "make all Laws which shall be necessary and proper for carrying into Execution the foregoing Powers, and all other Powers vested by this Constitution in the Government of the United States, or in any Department or Officer thereof."

The history of the Tenth Amendment underscores the legitimacy of implied powers. The Articles of Confederation protected state sovereignty by providing that states retained all powers except those "expressly delegated" to the national government. When that phrase was proposed in 1789 for the Tenth Amendment, to be included in the Bill of Rights, Madison objected to "expressly" because the functions and responsibilities of the new national government could not be delineated with such precision. It was impossible to confine a government to the exercise of express powers, for there "must necessarily be admitted powers by implication, unless the Constitution descended to recount every minutiae."[24] On the strength of his argument the word "expressly" was eliminated. Chief Justice Marshall relied on this legislative history in the great case of *McCulloch* v. *Maryland* when the Court upheld the power of Congress to establish a national bank, even though such power is not expressly included in the Constitution.[25]

The boundaries between the three branches of government are also strongly affected by the role of custom and acquiescence. When one branch engages in a certain practice and the other branches acquiesce, the practice gains legitimacy and can fix the meaning of the Constitution.[26] The President's power to remove officials was upheld in a 1903 ruling based largely on the "universal practice of the government for over a century."[27] Justice Frankfurter explained how executive power can grow when unchallenged: "A systematic, unbroken executive practice, long pursued to the knowledge of the Congress and never before questioned, engaged in by Presidents who have also sworn to uphold the Constitution, making as it were such exercise of power part of the structure of our government, may be treated as a gloss on 'executive Power' vested in the President by § 1 of Art. II."[28]

Creating The Executive Departments

The Constitution establishes only a shell for government. It was left to the first Congress, by statute, to create executive departments and federal courts. In so doing, it necessarily debated and decided a number of fundamental constitutional issues. At that time there was neither a judiciary nor judicial precedents, much less the practice (and acceptability) of judicial review. From 1789 to the present, it has been primarily the responsibility of Congress to determine the structure of government, the powers and functions of agencies, limitations on the President's power to remove executive officials, and the qualifications of appointees.

Since each department had to be created by statute, the first Congress could have placed departments under a single individual or a board of commissioners. The experience under the Articles of Confederation convinced most legislators that the board system lacked responsibility, energy, and order. The House of Representatives in 1789 voted for single executives to head the departments. Congress treated the Secretary of Foreign Affairs and the Secretary of War as purely executive officials, which had been the practice under the Articles. In contrast, Congress regarded the Secretary of the Treasury partly as a *legislative* agent, reflecting the mixed record during the Articles when the duties shifted back and forth between a Superintendent of Finance and a Board of Treasury. The first Secretary of the Treasury, Alexander Hamilton, performed essentially as an arm of the President, not Congress, and so it has been ever since.

Under President Andrew Jackson, Congress tried to treat the Secretary of the Treasury as a legislative agent. Jackson eventually prevailed in his argument that the Secretary is "wholly an executive officer," but he had to remove two Secretaries of the Treasury to effectuate his policy and was censured by the Senate for his action. Three years later the Senate ordered its resolution of censure expunged from the record.[29]

Some of the officers within the Treasury Department had duties that were not wholly executive in nature. During debate on the Department in 1789, Madison admitted that the comptroller's office "seemed to bear a strong affinity" to the legislative branch, while its settlement and adjustment of legal claims "partake too much of the Judicial capacity to be blended with the Executive."[30] When Congress created the General Accounting Office in 1921, it transferred to it not merely the powers and duties of the comptroller but even the personnel. GAO functions as a mixed agency. It is "legislative" when it audits accounts and investigates programs and "executive" when it approves payments and settles and adjusts accounts.[31]

This hybrid status was attacked by the Reagan administration in 1985 when it challenged the Comptroller General's authority to carry out spending cuts under the Gramm-Rudman-Hollings Act. The statute, which required federal deficits to decline to zero by fiscal 1991, authorized the Comptroller General under certain circumstances to order program cuts to be carried out by the President through a "sequestration" process. The administration claimed that Congress could not give executive duties to a legislative officer. In 1986 the Supreme Court agreed that the Comptroller General's sequestration duties were unconstitutional because Congress could not vest executive functions in an officer removable by Congress.[32] Nevertheless, the Comptroller General continues to carry out other functions of a quasi-executive and quasi-judicial nature.[33]

Another dispute concerns the President's authority to supervise the officers within the executive branch. A careless reading of the Constitution gives the President the power to execute the laws. In fact, he is to "take Care that the Laws be faithfully executed." What happens if a statute places the execution of a program outside his control? Does this violate the principle of responsibility and accountability vested in a single executive? The short answer is that the heads of executive departments function only in part as political agents of the President. They also perform legal duties assigned them by Congress. In *Marbury* v. *Madison*, Chief Justice John Marshall distinguished between two types of duties for a Cabinet head: ministerial and discretionary. The first allowed Congress to direct a Secretary to carry out certain activities. The second duty was owed to the President alone. When a Secretary performs the first duty he is bound to obey the laws: "He acts . . . under the authority of law, and not by the instructions of the President. It is a Ministerial act which the law enjoins for a particular purpose."[34]

The concept of ministerial duties reappears in *Kendall* v. *United States*. Congress could mandate that certain payments be made, and neither the head of the executive department nor the President could deny or control these ministerial acts.[35] In 1854 the Attorney General stated that when laws "define what is to be done by a given head of department, and how he is to do it, there the President's discretion stops . . . ."[36]

Appointments and Removals

Three steps are required to fill offices created by Congress: nomination by the President, confirmation by the Senate, and commissioning of the appointee by the President. For lesser officers, the Constitution permits Congress to dispense with the confirmation process and place the power of appointment directly in the President, the courts, or department heads.

In legal theory, the power to nominate is the "sole act of the president" and "completely voluntary."[37] Congress cannot designate the person to fill the office it creates.[38] Nevertheless, it can stipulate the qualifications of appointees, and legislators frequently select the names of judges, United States attorneys, and marshals for their state. In such cases the roles are reversed: Congress nominates and the President "advises and consents." If the names submitted by Congress are unacceptable, the White House and the Justice Department can object and request substitute proposals. Interest groups and professional organizations are also active in submitting names for consideration and evaluating those who are nominated.

There are limits to congressional intervention. In 1976 the Supreme Court reviewed a statute giving Congress the power to appoint four members to the Federal Election Commission, which monitors the financing and conduct of congressional and presidential elections. All six voting members (including two nominated by the President) required confirmation by the majority of *both* Houses of Congress. The Court ruled that Congress could not select officers responsible for carrying out executive and judicial duties. Such functions could be exercised only by "Officers of the United States" appointed pursuant to Art. II, 2, cl. 2. For the Court this meant either one of two constitutional options: nomination by the President, subject to the advice and consent of the Senate; or vesting the appointment power in the President alone, in the courts of law, or in department heads. Congress took the first option when it rewrote the statute. The decision explains how the appointment process is related to presidential responsibility and the separation doctrine.[39]

The framers recognized that the Senate would not always be in session to give advice and consent to presidential nominations. To cover these periods the President is authorized to make recess appointments "The President shall have power to fill up all Vacancies that may happen during the Recess of the Senate, by granting Commissions which shall expire at the End of their next Session." The word "happen" is interpreted broadly to mean "happen to exist," even if a vacancy occurred while the Senate was in session.[40] The meaning of "recess" remains uncertain, although the Justice Department agrees that adjournments "for 5 or even 10 days" are too short to justify the use of the recess power.[41]

In 1863, when it appeared that Presidents were abusing the power to make recess appointments and were deliberately circumventing the Senate's confirmation role, Congress passed legislation to prohibit the use of funds to pay the salary of anyone appointed during a Senate recess to fill a vacancy that existed "while the Senate was in session and is by law required to be filled by and with the advice and consent of the Senate, until such appointee shall have been confirmed by the Senate."[42] The law was liberalized in 1940 to permit payment under three conditions.[43] Legislation has also been passed to prohibit funds to pay the salary of any recess appointee who is later rejected by the Senate.[44]

Although the Constitution provides no express authority for the President to remove officials in the executive branch, it was agreed by the First Congress that responsible government required the President to dismiss incompetent, corrupt, or unreliable administrators. If anything by nature is executive, Madison said, "it must be that power which is employed in superintending and seeing that the laws are faithfully executed."[45]

These debates in 1789 were interpreted by Chief Justice Taft to leave not the "slightest doubt" that the power to remove officers appointed by the President and confirmed by the Senate is "vested in the President alone."[46] Taft reached too far; the debates reveal deep divisions among House members and close votes on the Senate side.[47] Moreover, the debates in 1789 focused on the President's power to remove the Secretary of Foreign Affairs, which Congress conceded to be an agent of the President and executive in nature. Madison anticipated other types of officers in the executive branch who might have a mix of legislative and judicial duties, requiring greater independence from the President.[48] Congress can place statutory limitations on the removal power, and the Supreme Court had recognized, before Taft made his sweeping claim, that Congress may identify the grounds for removal.[49]

A balance must be struck between the President's authority to remove executive officials and Congress' power under the Necessary and Proper Clause to create an office and attach conditions to it. Taft's decision was later modified to permit Congress to limit the President's power to remove commissioners with quasi-legislative and quasi-judicial powers.[50] Depending on statutory language or commitments by the President and his subordinates to maintain an officer's independence, presidential power to remove officers may face other constraints.[51]

Beyond the occasional lawsuit are the more frequent interventions by Congress. Congress may remove an individual by abolishing the office. A term of office created by one statute can be reduced or eliminated by a subsequent statute, requiring the discharge of a federal employee.[52] Through the passage of non-binding resolutions, committee investigations, the contempt power, and other pressures, Congress can precipitate a person's resignation or removal. Congress also intervenes to *protect* an officeholder, particularly a "whistleblower" who has alerted Congress to agency deficiencies. Members intervene for reasons of simple justice and to keep open the channels of communication between agencies and Congress.[53]

Delegation of Legislative Power

The boundaries between the legislative and executive branches are further obscured by the large grants of power delegated by Congress. This delegation supposedly violates a fundamental principle, dating back to John Locke. He said that the legislature "cannot transfer the power of making laws to any other hands, for it being but a delegated power from the people, they who have it cannot pass it over to others."[54] This principle is essential in preventing Congress from delegating its legislative power to private groups. In 1936 the Supreme Court struck down a statute partly because it delegated power to representatives of the coal industry to set up a code of mandatory regulations. The Court called this "legislative delegation in its most obnoxious form; for it is is not even delegation to an official or an official body, presumptively disinterested, but to private persons whose interests may be and often are adverse to the interests of others in the same business."[55]

With the exception of two cases handed down in 1935,[56] Congress has encountered little opposition from the courts in delegating legislative power to the President, executive agencies, and independent commissions. In sustaining these delegations, the judiciary typically waxes eloquent about the serious breach were Congress ever to transfer its legislative power to other parties, after which it finds a way to uphold the delegation.[57] The courts justify vast delegations of legislative power after satisfying themselves that the powers are confined either by congressional guidelines or procedural safeguards. At times these guidelines are found only in the legislative history and nonstatutory sources. Other restrictions are supplied by general statutes that establish standards for agency rulemaking to assure fairness and openness. The Administrative Procedure Act requires agencies to give notice and a hearing before issuing a rule or regulation. Findings of fact are supplied for the record; procedures exist for appeal. Through such procedural standards Congress tries to eliminate or minimize the opportunity for executive caprice and arbitrariness. The APA relies on the doctrine of separated powers by prohibiting investigative or prosecuting personnel from participating in agency adjudications.

The impact of implied powers is nowhere more evident than in the struggle for information. Although the Constitution does not expressly give Congress the power to investigate, the Supreme Court in 1927 announced that a legislative body "cannot legislate wisely or effectively in the absence of information respecting the conditions which the legislation is intended to affect or change."[58] Similarly, the Constitution does not expressly permit the President to withhold information from Congress, and yet in 1974 the Court decided that the President's interest in withholding information to protect confidentiality with his advisers is implied in the Constitution: "to the extent this interest relates to the effective discharge of a President's powers, it is constitutionally based."[59]

There is an inevitable collision when Congress attempts to carry out its investigative function and the President invokes executive privilege. Which branch should surrender to the other? Major confrontations require some type of compromise, prodded by Congress' power to punish for contempt and the judiciary's ability to steer both branches in the direction of an acceptable accommodation.

Congress relies on its investigative power to enact legislation, to oversee the administration of programs, to inform the public, and to protect its integrity, dignity, reputation, and privileges. To enforce each of these responsibilities, Congress possesses an inherent power to punish for contempt. Congress can also exercise this contempt power through the courts. If executive officials refuse congressional requests for information, a move by Congress to cite the person for contempt is often an effective way to get the official's attention and cooperation. In 1982 the House of Representatives voted 259 to 105 to hold Anne Gorsuch, administrator of the Environmental Protection Agency, in contempt. In an unprecedented action, the U.S. Attorney did not take the contempt citation to the grand jury, as required by statute. Instead, the administration asked a district court to declare the House action an unconstitutional intrusion into the President's authority to withhold information from Congress. The district judge bounced the ball back into the executive and legislative courts, telling them to devote their energies to compromise and cooperation, not confrontation. The documents were released to Congress.[60]

The major "executive privilege" case, *United States* v. *Nixon*, did not involve a congressional request for executive documents. The request came instead from the courts as part of the effort to prosecute Watergate crimes. A unanimous Court rejected the argument that the decision to release such documents is up to the President, not the courts. To permit Nixon absolute control over the documents would have prevented the judiciary from carrying out its duties.

Conflicts between the executive and legislative branches are usually worked out without litigation. Sometimes federal judges help the two sides find an acceptable accommodation. A deadlock between a House committee and the Justice Department during the 1970s, regarding the release of "national security" information, was eventually broken through the efforts of Circuit Judge Harold Leventhal, who convinced each branch that a compromise worked out between them would be better than a solution imposed by the courts. He put pressure on both parties to clarify their major concerns and reach an accommodation.[61]

Most of these conflicts between Congress and the President are resolved through informal negotiations and political compromise. Rarely does an issue enter the judicial arena. When it does, the courts are reluctant to set hard and fast rules in such complex areas as executive privilege, delegation, and congressional investigations. An emphasis is placed on middle-ground remedies that protect the essential interests of each branch. Beyond the statutory framework agreed to by executive and legislative officials, the two branches have evolved an elaborate system of informal, nonstatutory agreements that satisfy the conflicting demands of executive flexibility and congressional control.

This emphasis on informal agreements seems at odds with the command that this is a "government of laws and not of men." Although agencies are subject to authorization and appropriation actions through public law, much of the congressional control is maintained outside the statutory process. Committee reports, committee hearings, correspondence from review committees, and other nonstatutory techniques allow Congress to monitor and direct agency activity without passing another public law. Since these controls are informal and not legally binding, the system functions on a "keep the faith" attitude. Agencies receive lump-sum funds and broad authority from Congress; in return they acquiesce to a multitude of non-statutory controls. Agencies follow these controls for practical, not legal, reasons. Violations of congressional trust may result in budget cutbacks, restrictive statutory language, and line-item appropriations.

The Legislative Veto

This *quid pro quo* includes the "legislative veto." During the 1930s, executive officials wanted to "make law" without passage of a statute. President Hoover obtained authority to reorganize the executive branch without having to submit a bill to Congress for hearings, amendments, and enactment by both Houses. Congress agreed only on the condition that either House could reject a reorganization plan by passing a resolution of disapproval. Through this accommodation was born the legislative veto. Congress experimented with the one-House veto, the two-House veto (passage of a concurrent resolution), and even a committee veto.[62]

This procedure obviously departed from the Presentment Clause in Art. I, 7, which provides that "Every Order, Resolution, or Vote to which the Concurrence of the Senate and House of Representatives may be necessary (except on a question of Adjournment)" shall be presented to the President. Legislative vetoes were not presented to the President. President Hoover accepted the compromise because it simplified executive reorganization. This *quid pro quo* was extended to other areas, including immigration, arms sales, and impoundment of funds. Eventually the Justice Department and the White House decided that the bargain was no longer in the interest of the executive branch. A test case, involving an immigration statute, was soon on the way to the Supreme Court.

In the 1930s, the executive branch had prevailed upon Congress to delegate discretionary authority over the deportation of aliens. Congress agreed to allow the Attorney General to suspend deportations provided that the suspensions were subject to a legislative veto. Congress exercised this power on numerous occasions, but when it disapproved the suspension of deportation for six aliens in 1975, one was named Jagdish Rai Chadha. After exhausting his administrative remedies in the Immigration and Naturalization Service, he won a court victory in the Ninth Circuit in 1980. The Supreme Court granted certiorari and twice heard the case on oral argument.

In a sweeping decision in 1983, the Supreme Court declared the legislative veto unconstitutional because these forms of legislative action were not presented to the President for his signature or veto.

Some also violated the principle of bicameralism because they were acted upon by a single House. Chief Justice Burger, writing for the majority, said that whenever congressional action has the "purpose and effect of altering the legal rights, duties and relations of persons" outside the legislative branch, Congress must act through both Houses in a bill presented to the President.[63]

The Court's opinion suffers from a number of deficiencies. It claimed that the convenience of the legislative veto could not overcome the framers' view that efficiency was not a primary objective or hallmark of democratic government, and yet the framers ranked efficiency highly. The Court also argued that the legislative veto threatened the independence of the President by evading his veto power, but Presidents encouraged the legislative veto to obtain greater authority. Since under the legislative veto procedure Congress could not amend a President's proposal, the general veto was not needed for presidential self-defense.

More importantly, the decision did not, and could not, eliminate the conditions that gave rise to the legislative veto: the desire of executive officials for broad delegations of power, and the insistence of Congress that it control those delegations without having to pass another public law. The executive-legislative accommodations that prevailed before the Court's decision continue to exist, sometimes in forms that are indistinguishable from the legislative veto supposedly struck down to the Court. From the Court's decision on June 23, 1983, to the end of the 99th Congress in October 1986, Congress enacted more than a hundred new legislative vetoes, most of them of the committee variety.

The persistence of legislative vetoes can be illustrated by an incident that occurred in 1984. The housing appropriation bill passed by Congress contained a number of committee vetoes. In signing the bill into law, President Reagan took note of the legislative vetoes and asked Congress to stop adding provisions that the Supreme Court had already held to be unconstitutional. Moreover, he said that the administration did not regard the committee vetoes to be legally binding. As a consequence, agencies would merely notify the committees but would not seek their approval.[64]

In response, the House Appropriations Committee reconsidered a *quid pro quo* that it had made with the National Aeronautics and Space Administration (NASA). Dollar caps had been set on various NASA programs, usually at the level requested in the President's budget. The agreement allowed NASA to exceed the caps with the approval of the Appropriations Committees. Because of Reagan's threat to ignore committee controls, the House Appropriations Committee said that it would repeal both the committee veto and NASA's authority to exceed the dollar caps. If NASA needed to exceed those levels in the future, it would have to do what the Court said in *Chadha*: get a public law.[65]

NASA did not want to jump the entire legislative hurdle to make these mid-year adjustments. The Administrator of NASA, James M. Beggs, wrote to both Appropriations Committees and suggested a nonstatutory approach. His letter reveals the pragmatic sense of give-and-take that is customary between executive agencies and congressional committees. The letter also underscores the impracticality and unreality of the doctrines announced by the Supreme Court. Beggs proposed that future laws delete the committee veto and the dollar caps. The caps would be placed in the conference report accompanying the appropriations bill. In return, NASA would agree that it would not exceed those caps "without the prior approval of the Committees."[66] What could not be done directly by statute was achieved indirectly by informal agreement.

Chadha does not affect these nonstatutory "legislative vetoes." They are not legal in effect. They are, however, in effect legal. Agencies are aware of the penalties that Congress can invoke if they decide to violate understandings with their review committees.

Foreign Affairs

The doctrine of separated powers carries its share of subtleties and puzzles in domestic disputes. Even more problematic is the doctrine's application to external affairs and emergency powers. Those who believe that the lion's share of authority in foreign affairs belongs with the President rely heavily on Justice Sutherland's decision in *United States* v. *Curtiss-Wright*. The case could have been confined to a single question: may Congress delegate to the President the authority to prohibit the shipment of arms or munitions to any country in South America whenever he decided that the material would promote domestic violence? The Court agreed that legislation over the international field must often accord to the President greater discretion than would be admissible for domestic affairs. But Sutherland went beyond the issue of delegation to add pages of *obiter dicta* to describe the far-reaching dimensions of executive power in foreign affairs. He assigned to the President a number of powers not found in the Constitution. *Curtiss-Wright* is cited frequently to justify not only broad grants of legislative power to the President but the exercise of inherent and extraconstitutional powers.[67]

Curtiss-Wright echoed positions Sutherland had taken as a United States Senator and as a member of the Senate Foreign Relations Committee. It closely tracks his article "The Internal and External Powers of the National Government," printed as Senate Document No. 417 in 1910, which claimed that national power "inhered in the United States from the beginning" rather than in the colonies or the states. In his book, *Constitutional Power and World Affairs*,[68] he advanced the same themes.

The contemporary Supreme Court continues to look more sympathetically upon delegation that involves external affairs. Even Chief Justice Rehnquist, the strongest advocate of the nondelegation doctrine on the present Court, adopts a different standard for international crises, "the nature of which Congress can hardly have been expected to anticipate in any detail."[69] He agrees that Congress "is permitted to legislate both with greater breadth and with greater flexibility" when a statute governs military affairs.[70] More importantly, *Curtiss-Wright* is used to support the existence of independent, implied, and inherent powers for the President.[71]

Sutherland believed that foreign and domestic affairs were fundamentally different because the powers of external sovereignty passed from the Crown "not to the colonies severally, but to the colonies in their collective and corporate capacity as the United States of America." However, the colonies and states from 1774 to 1788 operated as sovereign entities, not as part of a collective body. They acted free and independent of one another. The creation of the Continental Congress did not disturb the sovereign capacity of the states to make treaties, borrow money, solicit arms, lay embargoes, collect tariff duties, and conduct separate military campaigns.

Even if the power of external sovereignty has somehow passed intact from the Crown to the "United States," the Constitution divides that power between Congress and the President. The President and the Senate share the treaty power. Because of the requirement for funds to implement treaties, the House of Representatives has come to participate more actively in this area of international agreements. Moreover, the Constitution gives Congress the power to raise and support the military forces, to lay and collect duties on foreign trade, and to regulate commerce with foreign nations. Contemporary conditions make it increasingly difficult to draw a crisp line between external and internal affairs. Oil embargoes imposed by foreign governments have an immediate impact on America's economy, raising the price at home and producing long lines at the neighborhood gas station. The President's decision to ship or withhold wheat from the Soviet Union has a major effect on farming communities. Trade policies are both international and domestic in scope.

Congress is given specific power to declare war, but Congress has declared war only five times. On all other occasions the President has entered into combat or hostilities without a declaration. As early as 1800 and 1801, the Supreme Court recognized the constitutionality of undeclared wars, which the Court called limited, partial, imperfect, or "quasi" wars.[72] The history of the past two centuries has been one of balancing and reconciling these two powers: war-declaring by Congress and war-making by the President.

The Constitution makes the President "Commander in Chief" of the armed forces. Scholars disagree whether this merely confers a title or implies additional powers for the President. Where the power begins or ends has mystified the courts.[73] The delegates at the Philadelphia Convention recognized an implied power for the President to "repel sudden attacks." When it was proposed that Congress be empowered to "make war," Charles Pinckney objected that legislative proceedings "were too slow" for the safety of the country in an emergency. Madison and Elbridge Gerry successfully inserted "declare" for "make," thereby "leaving to the Executive the power to repel sudden attacks."

The Supreme Court stated in 1850 that the President as commander in chief "is authorized to direct the movements of the naval and military forces placed by law at his command, and to employ them in the manner he may deem most effectual to harass and subdue the enemy."[74] But what is the power to move forces "placed by *law* at his command"? How much does the President depend on Congress to provide the authorizations and appropriations necessary for military action? Under the Constitution, it is the responsibility of Congress to raise and support the military forces, to make military regulations, to provide for calling up the militia to suppress insurrections and to repel invasions, and to provide for organizing and disciplining the militia.

These original allocations of power to Congress and the President have changed in the face of several developments. The idea of "defensive war" was initially limited to protective actions against the borders of the United States or naval wars against the Barbary pirates and France. After World War II, defensive war assumed a much broader meaning. American bases were spread throughout the world; commitments were added to defense pacts and treaties. Under these agreements an attack on an ally became an attack on the United States. Presidents also used military force on numerous occasions to protect American lives and property, often stretching those objectives to achieve foreign policy or military objectives. Examples include the Dominican Republic in 1965, Cambodia in 1970, and Grenada in 1983. The bombing of Libya in 1986 was defended as an anti-terrorist response. The selling of arms to Iran has been justified by President Reagan for a number of reasons, in part to obtain the release of American hostages.

Congress has enacted a number of statutes to place controls on military activities. The purpose of the CIA statute in 1980 was to keep the House and Senate Intelligence Committees informed of covert actions, but obviously the intent of this law has been circumvented by executive officials. The Boland amendments were enacted to prohibit direct or indirect assistance to the Contras in Nicaragua. Evidently these laws, and perhaps others, have been broken. The purpose of the War Powers Resolution of 1973 was to insure the "collective judgment" of both branches before introducing U.S. forces into hostilities, and yet administrative officials argue that the President has a number of constitutional powers that enable him to use military force without bothering to consult with Congress, much less seek its approval.

Although the War Powers Resolution has been criticized as unworkable and an encroachment on presidential responsibilities, there is greater appreciation in contemporary times that presidential military actions must have the support and understanding of Congress. As a post-mortem on the Vietnam war, Secretary of State Henry Kissinger offered this perspective in 1975: "Comity between the executive and legislative branches is the only possible basis for national action. The decade-long struggle in this country over executive dominance in foreign affairs is over. The recognition that the Congress is a coequal branch of government is the dominant fact of national politics today. The executive accepts that the Congress must have both the sense and the reality of participation: foreign policy must be a shared enterprise."[75] The "collective judgment" contemplated in the War Powers Resolution is an essential condition for creating and sustaining effective policies in military and foreign affairs.

The decision by members of the Reagan White House and other administration officials to provide military assistance to rebels in Nicaragua, despite a congressional ban on such aid, produced the first serious crisis for the Reagan administration. The cooperative and consultative attitude, so effective in the early years of this administration, gave way to a policy of exclusion, not only of Congress but of the Joint Chiefs of Staff, the Defense Department, the State Department, and other agencies that were less than enthusiastic about the Iran-Contra policy. These unilateral and probably illegal actions have also created doubt among American allies regarding the President's ability to operate the White House, manage foreign policy, and develop the necessary support for his policies from Congress and the people.

In the Steel Seizure Case of 1952, Justice Jackson developed a theory of extraconstitutional powers that had three scenarios. Presidential authority reaches its highest level when the President acts pursuant to congressional authorization, for here he operates not only with his own panoply of powers but with Congress' as well. His power is at its "lowest ebb" when he takes measures incompatible with the will of Congress, which was the choice of the Reagan White House. But in between these two categories lay a "zone of twilight" in which Congress neither grants nor denies authority. In such circumstances, "congressional inertia, indifference or quiescence may sometimes, at least as a practical matter, enable, if not invite, measures of independent presidential responsibility."[76]

Jackson's opinion underscores the fact that the Constitution is shaped not merely by textual interpretations from the courts but by a political dialectic between the executive and legislative branches. Under the *Curtiss-Wright* model, the President is blessed with extraconstitutional, inherent powers. The necessities of international affairs and diplomacy make the President the dominant figure. On the other hand, the Steel Seizure Case assumes that Congress is the basic lawmaker in both domestic and foreign affairs. Inherent powers are denied, although congressional inertia, silence, or acquiescence may invite independent and conclusive actions by the President.

The lesson to be drawn from either model is that Congress has ample powers to legislate for emergencies, at home and abroad, but those powers must be exercised. Congressional influence depends on its willingness to act and to take responsibility. Presidential influence, at least for commitments of a long-term nature, cannot survive on assertions of inherent power. The President needs the support and understanding of both Congress and the public.

How much Congress asserts itself, and how much the President stays in touch with public attitudes, depends to a crucial extent on our own willingness to follow national policy and voice our opinions. That is the essence of self-government, and no better time exists for putting it into practice than this year, the year of our bicentennial.

Endnotes

1. Louis Fisher, *President and Congress* (New York: Free Press, 1972), 1–27, 253–270 (1972).
2. Id. at 16.
3. Sidney Teiser, "The Genesis of the Supreme Court," 25 *Virginia Law Review* 398 (1939); F. Regis Noel, "Vestiges of a Supreme Court Among the Colonies and Under the Articles of Confederation," *Records Columbia Historical Society*, Vol. 37–38, p. 123 (1937).
4. 1 Francis Wharton, *The Revolutionary Correspondence of the United States* (Washington: Government Printing Office, 1889), 663.
5. *Myers* v. *United States*, 272 U.S. 52, 293 (1926).
6. Louis Fisher, "The Efficiency Side of Separated Powers," 5 *Journal of American Studies* 113 (1971).
7. M.J.C. Vile, *Constitutionalism and the Separation of Powers* (Oxford: Clarendon Press, 1967), 176–211.
8. 1 Joseph Story, *Commentaries on the Constitution of the United States* (Boston: Hilliard Grey and Co., 1905), 396.
9. *Youngstown Co.* v. *Sawyer*, 343 U.S. 579, 635 (1952).
10. *Schlesinger* v. *Reservists to Stop the War*, 418 U.S. 208 (1974).
11. 1 Max Farrand, *The Records of the Federal Convention* (New Haven: Yale University Press, 1911), 379–382, 386–390; 2 Farrand 283–284, 489–492.
12. 43 *Congressional Record* 2390–2404, 2408–2415 (1909); 35 Stat. 626 (1909).
13. 87 Stat. 697 (1973).
14. 119 *Congressional Record* 37688–37690, 38315–38349, 39234–39246 (1973).
15. *United States* v. *Will*, 449 U.S. 200 (1980).
16. *United States* v. *Brewster*, 408 U.S. 501, 507 (1972).
17. *Kennedy* v. *Sampson*, 511 F.2d 430 (D.C. Cir. 1974); *Wright* v. *United States*, 302 U.S. 583 (1938). See also *The Pocket Veto Case*, 279 U.S. 644 (1929).
18. *Barnes* v. *Kline*, 759 F.2d 21 (D.C. CIr. 1985); *Barens* v. *Carmen*, 582 F.Supp. 163 (D.D.C. 1984). On January 14, 1987, in *Burke* v. *Barnes*, the Supreme Court held that this case was moot and therefore no longer a case or controversy to be decided.
19. 3 Jonathan Elliot, *Debates in the Several State Conventions on the Adoption of the Federal Constitution* (Philadelphia: J.B. Lippincott, 1863–91), 280.

20. 4 Id. 116, 121; John Bach McMaster and Frederick D. Stone, eds., *Pennsylvania and the Federal Constitution* (New York: Appleton-Century, 1888), 475–477 (1888).

21. 1 *Annals of Congress* 453 (1789). See also Edward Dumbauld, *The Bill of Rights and What It Means Today* (Norman, Okla.: Oklahoma University Press, 1957), 174–175, 183, 199.

22. Vile, *Constitutionalism and the Separation of Powers* 153.

23. 1 U.S. Senate, *Journals* 64, 73–74 (1820); 1 *Annals of Congress* 435–436, 789–790 (1789).

24. 1 *Annals of Congress* 761 (1789).

25. 17 U.S. (4 Wheat.) 315 (1819).

26. *Stuart* v. *Laird*, 5 U.S. (1 Cr.) 299, 309 (1803).

27. *Shurtleff* v. *United States*, 189 U.S. 311, 316 (1903). See also *United States* v. *Midwest Oil Co.*, 236 U.S. 459, 469–471 (1915).

28. *Youngstown Co.* v. *Sawyer*, 343 U.S. at 610–611.

29. Louis Fisher, *Constitutional Conflicts between Congress and the President* (Princeton: Princeton University Press, 1985), 67–68.

30. 1 *Annals of Congress* 613, 614 (1789).

31. *United States ex rel. Brookfield Const. Co., Inc.* v. *Stewart*, 234 F.Supp. 94, 99–100 (D.D.C. 1964), aff'd, 339 F.2d 754 (D.C. Cir. 1964).

32. 106 S.Ct. 3181 (1986).

33. *Ameron, Inc.* v. *U.S. Army Corps of Engineers*, 607 F.Supp. 962 (D. N.J. 1985); *Ameron, Inc.* v. *U.S. Army Corps of Engineers*, 610 F.Supp. 750 (D. N.J. 1985); *Ameron, Inc.* v. *U.S. Army Corps of Engineers*, 787 F.2d 875 (3d Cir. 1986); *Ameron, Inc.* v. *U.S. Army Corps of Engineers*, 809 F.2d 979 (3d Cir. 1986).

34. 5 U.S. (1 Cr.) 137, 162 (1803).

35. 37 U.S. 522 (1838).

36. 6 Op. Att'y Gen. 326, 341 (1854).

37. 5 U.S. at 155.

38. *United States* v. *Ferreira*, 54 U.S. (13 How.) 39, 50–51 (1852); *Myers* v. *United States*, 272 U.S. at 128.

39. *Buckley* v. *Valeo*, 424 U.S. 1 (1976). 40. 1 Op. Att'y Gen. 631 (1823).

41. 3 Op. Att'y Gen. 20, 25 (1921); 3 O.L.C. 311, 314 (1979).

42. 12 Stat. 646 (1863).

43. 54 Stat. 751 (1940); 5 U.S.C. 5503 (1982).

44. E.g., 93 Stat. 574, 604 (1979); Fisher, *Constitutional Conflicts between Congress and the President*, 47–59.

45. 1 *Annals of Congress* 500 (1789).

46. *Myers* v. *United States*, 272 U.S. at 114.

47. Fisher, *Constitutional Conflicts between Congress and the President*, 61–66.
48. 1 *Annals of Congress* 611–614 (1789).
49. *Shurtleff* v. *United States*, 189 U.S. 311 (1903).
50. *Humphrey's Executor* v. *United States*, 295 U.S. 602 (1935); *Wiener* v. *United States*, 357 U.S. 349 (1958).
51. *Nader* v. *Bork*, 366 F.Supp. 104 (D.D.C. 1973).
52. *Crenshaw* v. *United States*, 134 U.S. 99 (1890).
53. Louis Fisher, "Congress and the Removal Power," 10 *Congress & the Presidency* 63 (1983).
54. John Locke, *Second Treatise on Civil Government*, 141.
55. *Carter* v. *Carter Coal Co.*, 298 U.S. 238, 311 (1936).
56. *Panama Refining Co.* v. *Ryan*, 293 U.S. 388 (1935); *Schechter Corp.* v. *United States*, 295 U.S. 495 (1935).
57. *Field* v. *Clark*, 143 U.S. 649, 692 (1891); *Hampton & Co.* v. *United States*, 276 U.S. 394, 406 (1928).
58. *McGrain* v. *Daugherty*, 273 U.S. 135, 175 (1927).
59. *United States* v. *Nixon*, 418 U.S. 683, 711 (1974).
60. *United States* v. *House of Representatives*, 556 F.Supp. 150 (D.D.C. 1983).
61. *United States* v. *ATT&T*, 567 F.2d 121 (D.C. Cir. 1977).
62. Fisher, *Constitutional Conflicts between Congress and the President*, 162–174.
63. *INS* v. *Chadha*, 462 U.S. 919 (1983).
64. 20 Wkly Comp. Pres. Doc. 1040 (July 18, 1984).
65. H. Rept. No. 916, 98th Cong., 2d Sess. 48 (1984).
66. Letter from NASA Administrator James M. Beggs to the House and Senate Appropriations Committees, August 9, 1984.
67. 299 U.S. 304 (1936).
68. George Sutherland, *Constitutional Power* (New York: Columbia University Press, 1919).
69. *Dames* v. *Moore*, 453 U.S. 654, 669 (1981).
70. *Rostker* v. *Goldberg*, 453 U.S. 57, 66 (1981), quoting *Parker* v. *Levy*, 417 U.S. 733, 756 (1974).
71. *United States* v. *Pink*, 315 U.S. 203, 229 (1942); *Knauff* v. *Shaughnessy*, 338 U.S. 537, 542 (1950); *United States* v. *Mazurie*, 419 U.S. 544, 566–567 (1975).
72. *Bas* v. *Tingy*, 4 U.S. (4 Dall.) 36 (1800); *Talbot* v. *Seeman*, 5 U.S. (1 Cr.) 1 (1801).
73. *Youngstown Co.* v. *Sawyer*, 343 U.S. at 641.
74. *Fleming* v. *Page*, 50 U.S. (9 How.) 602, 614 (1850).
75. 72 *Department of State Bulletin* 562 (1975).
76. *Youngstown Co.* v. *Sawyer*, 343 U.S. at 637.

Some Bicentennial Thoughts About Congress: Then, Now and in the Future

by

Michael J. Malbin
Minority Staff Consultant
Select Committee to Investigate
Covert Arms Transactions With Iran
U.S. House of Representatives

Adjunct Scholar
The American Enterprise Institute for Public Policy Research
Washington, D.C.

George Mason played an important role in the Constitutional Convention during the summer of 1787, but in the end refused to sign the document. Most Virginians know that Mason was upset that the Constitution did not contain a Bill of Rights. But Mason also objected to what the document had to say about Congress. The legislative body, Mason said in objections written at the end of the convention, would provide "not the substance, but only the shadow of representation."[1] This serious charge formed the heart of the Anti-Federalist critique of the Constitution. Mason ended up on the losing side in 1787–88, but his arguments still need to be taken seriously.

Today's Congress sometimes seems to be everybody's favorite whipping boy. The institution is charged with being too concerned with local interests, too fragmented internally, and too susceptible to interest group pressure. In some ways, today's criticism is the opposite of Mason's. Today's criticism is not that Congress fails to reflect the people but, on the contrary, that it responds too much to immediate pressures and therefore is unable to make policy. Which criticism is closer to reality, Mason's or the more modern one? Both capture a partial truth, but both are also profoundly wrong. Congress is concerned with local interests; it is fragmented; it is susceptible to interest group pressure. The real question is not whether it is all these things, but whether it is too much so. This essay will address this concern in the following order:

First, the framers of the Constitution expected, intended and even desired some localism among House members; they also expected and encouraged a proliferation of interest groups around the country.

Second, even though the framers expected and wanted factionalism, they also wanted outside pressures to be counterbalanced by a set of incentives *within* Congress that would promote deliberation in the name of the common good.

Third, over the years, the forces supporting fragmentation in Congress have become stronger, but the forces meant to promote deliberation have become weaker.

Fourth, in coming decades, technology is likely to accelerate present trends, making deliberation during the Constitution's third century just that much more difficult.

The fifth and final point concerns reform. A number of people who have looked at recent trends think the Constitution needs to be revised radically to create something more like a parliamentary system. These proposals are misguided. Whatever problems exist with the present system, the Constitution looks good when compared to the realistic alternatives.

The Framers' Intentions

More than half of the recorded debates at the Constitutional Convention were about Congress. As important as these specific debates were, however, we can*not* understand Congress unless we first talk about broader questions.

The main issue in the constitutional convention was whether there should be a national government at all. Obviously, the framers decided that by saying yes. When it made this decision, the convention took the single most important step it could have taken to constitute a country whose people would have a wide variety of economic and other interests. "The latent causes of faction" may be "sown in the nature of man," as James Madison said in *Federalist* 10,[2] but the large, commercial republic encouraged faction—deliberately. The purpose of diversification was not to prevent action as such. For that, the delegates could have stayed with the Articles of Confederation. Rather, diversity was meant to make certain *kinds* of decisions more difficult and less likely.

Why did the framers want to promote diversity? The reason was *not*, despite what many people say about checks and balances, to make it hard for the government to act. If that were all the framers had wanted, they could have stayed with the Articles of Confederation. The framers were trying to steer between two poles. They wanted a government strong enough to provide for the common defense and to promote interstate commerce. At the same time, they wanted to avoid the dangers of class warfare and religious warfare.

The framers thought that a large country and a vibrant economy would produce citizens more concerned with their private rights, and with preventing the government from usurping those rights, than with trying to gain control over the government to impose a single point of view or a single class interest on the whole country.

The more factions there are, the more difficult it would be to form any majority so single-minded that it would be willing to use its position to oppress a minority. People who want to be part of a governing majority in a large, diverse country are almost forced by the arithmetic of coalition building to think about other people's needs if they want to achieve their own objectives. Legislative majorities will have to be made up of coalitions of minorities that come together only after a process of accommodation and compromise. Factions that help form today's legislative majority will have to moderate their demands, both because their coalition partners will demand it of them, and because the politics of coalition may find them part of tomorrow's minority. For the same reason, today's minorities will not feel so frustrated as to think of rebellion, because they might well help form tomorrow's majority.

If diversity and commerce turn the government away from salvation and revolution, what do they turn the government toward? One obvious possibility was that the government would have avoided a very serious political danger for one that was less serious, but still problematic. A people devoted to the private pursuit of happiness would naturally try to have the government serve their own private purposes.

The framers believed most voters in a liberal democracy would be concerned primarily with their immediate well being. Much of their discussion of Congress was about how best to counter this tendency within a framework in which private interests are encouraged to develop. The Federalists were not interested in solutions that would work against the diversification of private interest because that would mean courting the dangers of polarization and civil war.

So the framers saw factional diversity as a good thing. As a price of encouraging this good thing, they were willing to accept the *inevitability* of factional, or special interest, influence in politics and government. The Federalists believed, contrary to some Whig writers of the 1770s,[3] that no amount of education or civic virtue could ever produce a body of citizens so united in their opinions, and so motivated by a common passion for the public good, that the problem of faction would simply disappear. "Liberty is to faction, what air is to fire," wrote Madison.[4] Human beings *by nature* will have different passions, opinions and interests. Even if all citizens could be made to care about the common good, they would not all have the same opinions. Inevitably, their opinions will be colored by their self love, no matter how virtuous their intentions. And opinions, once formed, will lead to faction, coalition and political action.

But the framers also believed that a successful government had to transcend faction to work for the common good. How did the framers hope to achieve this? The one way they refused to proceed was by trying to make sure virtuous politicians would always be in office. If self-love were bound to affect the perceptions of citizens, so too would it be bound to creep into the halls of government. "It is vain to say that enlightened statesmen will be able to adjust these clashing interests and render them all subservient to the public good," wrote Madison in *Federalist* 10. Enlightened statesmen will not always be at the helm.[5] When they designed the institutions of government, therefore, the framers thought it would be safer to assume that public officials would act out of self-interest. To that extent, their perspective looks a bit like the public choice theory used by many of George Mason University's economists. The framers differed from these contemporary theorists, though, in the breadth of their view of self-interest. Their argument, in truncated form, was:

(1) that self-interest involves a complicated set of passions;

(2) that people who seek political office often define their self-interest in terms of ambition or love of honor, as well as material well being; and

(3) that institutions can be shaped to encourage, control and then channel ambition toward politically desirable ends.

Channelling Ambition Through Institutions

It is well known that the framers relied on ambition for the separation of powers. People would protect their own offices as long as they had independent power bases for standing up to potential usurpers. "Ambition must be made to counteract ambition," said *Federalist* 51. "The interest of the man must be connected to the constitutional rights of the place."[6] Perhaps less well known is how the self-interest of politicians pervaded the framers' analysis of governmental institutions.

Consider how the framers looked at the issue political scientists now describe as "candidate recruitment." No legislature would ever withstand constituency pressures if all of its members' perspectives simply matched those of the voters. The framers did believe in democracy. They wanted Congress to be responsive to the public will. But they did not think they had to worry about that: responsiveness comes with the democratic turf. The difficult task was to combine responsiveness with some perspective. One precondition for perspective was a legislature at least some of whose members had ambitions or concerns larger than the district, as well as the ability to act on those ambitions of concerns competently.

During the Revolutionary War, Congress was made up of an impressive collection of delegates. As historian Jack Rakove has written, "attendance at Congress [during the war] was ... an obligation to be discharged, not an ambition to be fulfilled."[7] Afterwards, however, the day's leading political figures were no longer willing to serve. With no emergency, and a weak Confederation Congress, many of them preferred going back to their state legislatures. Said Alexander Hamilton: it became "difficult to find men who were willing to suffer the mortification to which so feeble a government, and so dependent a station, exposed them."[8]

The most important step the convention took to attract able people to Congress was to make the national government more powerful. Next, they turned to the selection process itself. The convention wanted to give the edge to the kind of Representatives and Senators they hoped would serve. For the House, large districts—about 30,000 people to start, or ten times as populous as a good-sized state legislative district of the day—were thought to favor people with earned reputations over those who might simply buy their elections through friendships and bribery. As for the Senate, indirect elections would work even better than district size by itself. Whatever else state legislators would look for when they elected a Senator, it was assumed they would want someone competent to represent the state's interests in the national legislature.

But persuading able people to serve can do only so much. The problem with which the framers' were grappling was to get Congress to rise above the factional diversity the framers knew the Constitution would stimulate. Competent people, by definition, would be smart enough to figure out how best to serve their own interests. If local factions were the only source of rewards and honor, politicians would see that and behave accordingly. The ones who tried to do otherwise would quickly find themselves out of office.

So the trick was to create incentives that persuade at least some members to look beyond their own districts' immediate passions. That gets to the second point of the outline: how did the framers try to create incentives *within* Congress to counter the effects of factional pressures from outside? Everyone knows that elected officials have a self-interest in serving the people who put them in office. The problem was how to get Congress to rise above constituency service as their only basis for action. They used six major devices to achieve these results. These devices had to do with (1) the length of congressional terms, (2) the scope of the national agenda, (3) the size of congressional districts, (4) the size of the legislature, (5) the way legislators would gain power within Congress and (6) how politicians would advance from one office to the next.

Length of Congressional Terms

The framers made congressional terms longer than the terms most people were used to at the time. Two years terms may seem short today, but ten states had one year terms for their lower houses in 1787, two had six month terms, and only one had a two year term. Two year House and six year Senate terms were supposed to give members of Congress some "breathing room" to stand up to the short term wishes of their own constituents. The framers thought two year terms would keep the House on a fairly short democratic leash, but would also give unpopular policies at least a little time to work and thus give the voters some chance for second thoughts before the next election. Six year Senate terms were meant to create even more breathing room for the body that was intended to be the government's repository of deliberative statesmanship. For both chambers, said Fisher Ames in the Massachusetts state ratifying convention, the idea was to let time work to allow "the sober, second thought of the people" to become law, instead of the passionate "volcano" of their "fiery" first impressions.[9]

Two year House and six year Senate terms were also supposed to serve another important purpose. By cutting down on the need for travel back home for annual elections, several convention delegates said they hoped members of Congress would feel less harried and therefore spend more time living in the capital. The aim was to create personal and working relationships among members, apart from the home district or state. How two year terms help achieve this was explained by Theodore Sedgwick of Massachusetts, later the President *pro tempore* of the U.S. Senate (1798) and Speaker of the House (6th Congress, 1799–1801). Speaking at the Massachusetts ratifying convention, Sedgwick said it would take more than a year for a representative to "divest himself of local concerns."[10] Representatives will need two years to shed local attachments and adopt at least something of a national perspective. They will need time to live among, talk to, and get to know their colleagues—time to learn the interests of the other states as their fellow legislators see them. Only if the representatives adopt this perspective will it be possible for them to combine their interests and pass complex legislation that may in fact serve the national interest. The perspective of 1787 thus was the reverse of the one put forward today by those who believe the government wears Washington blinders and ignores the rest of the country. The issue seen two hundred years ago was how to build a common set of experiences, and a common sense of purpose, among people whose strongest ties would be local.

The Deliberative Congress

The concern about building a common sense of purposes tied directly to the way the framers hoped Congress would work. Diversity was supposed to make it all but impossible for members simply to vote raw policy preferences up or down. The need to forge majorities out of diverse factions would force bargaining and compromise. At a minimum, legislative bargaining should help to moderate policy decisions. At its best, though, deliberation can rise above mechanical split-the-difference compromising to produce serious discussions among people with different interests, from different backgrounds, each genuinely trying to serve a national, rather than a series of parochial interests.

Why did the framers think discussion and deliberation were important to a legislative body? The reasons was *not* that two, four, or even 435, heads are always better than one. More heads need not mean better answers. Where speed and energy are important, the framers thought one head was better than two. Even if speed were not an issue, one expert is better than two lay people on many technical issues. But legislators are not merely technicians. Legislative deliberation, therefore, cannot be a solitary activity. Oliver Ellsworth made this point well when he told the constitutional convention, during a debate over whether to require annual sessions of Congress: "The Legislature will not know till they are met whether the public interest required their meeting or not."[11]

Group discussions are needed for legislative deliberation for at least three different reasons. *First,* as Ellsworth was saying, members cannot know without meeting whether problems in one district occur elsewhere too. *Second,* the members will disagree about ends—about what the government should try to achieve—as well as about means; they therefore cannot limit themselves to a search for the one best technique. *Finally,* in a democratic republic, it is just as important to gauge what is acceptable as to know what an expert says will work. If a significant number of people disagree with what an office holder wants to do, the Constitution is designed to force the office holder either to give up, or to persuade the people to change their opinions. Deciding when to give up and when to persuade is the essence of democratic leadership.

The remaining five devices of the six listed at the beginning of this discussion all relate directly to the desire to promote deliberation in Congress. The second device used—or, more accurately, assumed—by the framers to encourage deliberation in Congress had to do with the scope of the national agenda. The framers assumed Congress would devote its energies to a few major issues at a time. With a relatively limited agenda, Congress could stay in session only a few months of each year, and policies in fact would have some time to work before the next election. In addition, as long as the agenda was small, the members could engage in careful deliberation in the Committee of the Whole House or Senate without relying on specialized committees to predigest the issues. Finally, average voters could keep reasonably good track of what the government was doing and make their election judgments after hearing the policy arguments.

The third device had to do with the size of congressional districts and, like the last one, had to do with congressional elections. Districts in the First Congress had about 33,000 people. That may seem small to us, but was very large for the day. Only the country's two largest cities, New York and Philadelphia, had enough people in 1790 (about 30,000 each) to warrant a full representative. Boston's population was about 18,000, Charleston's was 16,000 and Baltimore's about 13,000. No other city reached 10,000.

Of course, 90 percent of the population lived outside cities in 1790. In a sense, this only increased the distance between representatives and their constituents. South Carolina's state legislature had a 110 member lower house and a 39 member upper house, but only five representatives to the U.S. Congress in 1789. The smallest state legislature was Delaware's, with 21 in the lower house and 9 in the upper; Delaware had one U.S. representative. The largest delegation to the first Congress was Virginia's at 10. Virginia's own lower house had 180 members and its upper house had 24. Each member of the U.S. House of Representatives, in other words, was expected to represent many more people than state legislators in even the smallest of the country's upper chambers. So Anti-Federalists had some real reason to wonder when they heard the House described as the most democratic branch of the national government. Districts made up of 30,000 people were a real departure, let alone the larger districts that would obviously come later.

This became one of the main points in the Anti-Federalists' critique of the Constitution during the ratification debates. How could one person know, let alone represent, the concerns of the whole city of Philadelphia, or a half dozen rural counties? "Our federal representatives," said George Mason in the Virginia state ratifying convention, "must be unacquainted with the situation of their constituents. Sixty-five members cannot possible know the situation and circumstances of all the inhabitants of this immense continent."[12]

That was why Mason called Congress unrepresentative: he thought small districts essential for controlling public officials. But the Federalists wanted districts to be large for at least two reasons. One was mentioned earlier: the Federalists thought large districts would favor the election of able people to Congress. The other was that large districts would have a variety of people, forcing elected members to build coalitions of factions to win an election. By making elections turn on coalition politics, the idea was to make legislators more free to pursue deliberative compromises than they would be if their careers were entirely beholden to the single interests that dominated the small state legislative districts of the day.

The fourth item was the size of the legislature itself. Large districts automatically would mean small chambers, but the framers wanted relatively small size chambers for another reason. Madison wrote in *Federalist 55* that the House should be large enough to insure "free consultation and discussion," but not so large as to produce the "confusion and intemperance of a multitude."[13] What would be too large in their eyes is something we do not know. The *Federalist* confidently predicted a house with 400 members.[14] But at some point, too large a legislature would produce the form of democratic control without the content. The actual result would be demagogic leadership by a few. "In all very numerous assemblies," Madison continued in No. 55, "passion never fails to wrest the scepter from reason. Had every Athenian citizen been a Socrates, every Athenian assembly would still have been a mob."[15] An excessively large assembly would enhance the constituents' views, in other words, but would do so by enlarging the flames of immediate passion. That is not what the convention delegates wanted from the Congress.

So the Federalists' concern about size grew directly out of their desire to promote deliberation. This in turn rested on a markedly different view of representation than the Anti-Federalist notion that a good representative is one who most closely reflects the views of his constituents. For the Federalists, a perfect mirroring is impossible; legislatures inevitably distort. Therefore, the real effort should be to distort through deliberation rather than demagogy. One way is by keeping the size of Congress within bounds. (This argument about size may be one explanation for the fact that deliberation in the contemporary Congress occurs more in committees and other small groups than in the full chamber.)

The fifth item had to do with how members would gain power within the House or Senate. Under the procedures of the early House and Senate, bills were considered and approved in principle by the Committee of the Whole before they were sent to a select committee to be put into legislative language. The framers thought this structure in a small body with a limited agenda would create a situation in which leadership was based not upon formal position or upon demagogy but upon the respect a member gained from his colleagues. This respect, they felt, could be gained in the full chamber *only* by members who were willing to break away from their immediate constituencies and take a broader perspective to promote compromises that looked to their colleagues' needs as well as their own. In practice, this meant that the real leader of the first House was not the Speaker, Frederick Muhlenberg, but a person who held no formal post—James Madison. House members looked to Madison partly because of his abilities, but also because the institution encouraged the members to seek deliberative rather than partisan or demagogic solutions to the issues before them.

The sixth and final method for promoting deliberation had to do with the way members would advance from one office to the next. The House was the only part of the federal government that was to be elected directly by the people. All other federal offices, including the Senate and Presidency, were filled by appointment or indirect election. That means no House member could advance to another federal office without first winning support from political peers. In other words, what members would have to do to exercise leadership within the chamber, and what they would do to move up to another office, were pretty much the same thing: both involved adopting a perspective would force the member to look beyond the local constituency to think more broadly.

Two Hundred Years Later

Obviously Congress has changed a great deal over the past two hundred years. We cannot review the history of congressional change in this essay. Instead, let us turn to how the contemporary Congress measures up to the framers' intentions on just a few of the six points just summarized, concentrating on the scope of the national agenda, the length of congressional terms and how people advance from one office to another.

Two year cycles originally were meant to give members of Congress some breathing room from constituency pressures. That is not how they have worked out. The reasons have to do with the growth of the governmental and legislative agendas, and with the longer cycle of election campaigning.

The delegates to the 1787 convention thought two year House terms would give Congress plenty of time for its legislative work. One of the delegates, General C.C. Pinckney, even told the South Carolina state ratifying convention that he thought congressional sessions would last only two or three months per year.[16] But the agenda grew over Congress's first century, and sessions became longer. After the New Deal (or maybe, as the most recent Republican Speaker, Joseph Martin, once said, it was after air conditioning made Washington bearable during the heat.[17]) Congress became an overloaded, year-round institution.

Today's Congress routinely has bills stacked up at the end of each cycle. What results is anything but the cautiously deliberative process the people of 1787 thought two years would allow. Because most members want to get home for the election campaign, the log-jam gives a handful of members a potent weapon—the threat to delay adjournment—to use against bills they oppose. Bills end up passing or failing because of parliamentary maneuvers that favor determined minorities.

A majority can defeat these end-game tactics if there is a strong enough consensus that a particular bill has to pass. Appropriations bills or omnibus continuing resolutions almost always are treated as "must" bills. The political mood usually favors a few other items each year. But even passing "must" bills has a price, as the last supporters needed to put a bill over the top can use the calendar to demand a stiff *quid pro quo* before they say yes.

So the scope of the national agenda clearly affects the way the two-year cycle works inside Congress. It also affects the relationships between members and their constituents, which is especially easy to see when looking at election campaigns. At the constitutional convention, one year terms were rejected because they would require members to engage in a permanent campaign. But that is exactly what the two year cycle means for many House members today. From the moment freshmen hit Washington, they busily cultivate their new constituencies to prepare for the next Election Day. Serious challengers and open seat candidates also routinely run campaigns that last at least eighteen months. It can take that long under the post–1974 campaign finance laws to raise the half million dollars or so the average winning challenger spends on a successful campaign. Over the past ten years, some challengers have even begun to adopt a four year game plan, using one election to weaken incumbents and establish their own credibility in the hope of winning the next time around.

Proposals abound to address these concerns by lengthening congressional terms to three or four years. There is no way to make such a change, however, without either changing the terms of senators and presidents, or radically altering the relationships among the separate branches. In fact, most people who propose four year House terms do so with the explicit intention of strengthening the President's political control over Congress. This issue will be addressed briefly in the conclusion.

Elections and Campaigning

Underlying the argument about term lengths during the ratification period was a shared agreement among Federalists and Anti-Federalists that voters should and would consider a legislator's record to help them decide whether they wanted the legislator to continue in office. Modern campaigns look like a caricature ·of this shared assumption.

Today's incumbents do everything they can to avoid being judged on the substantive policies they have helped enact or defeat. The average House members spends more than $1 million every two years to become better known by their constituents.[18] Some of this money is spent to explain the incumbent's positions on major national issues, but a great deal goes to project the incumbent as a person who can get jobs for the district, or who can help ordinary people straighten out problems with the bureaucracy. In addition, most House members outside large, metropolitan areas are able to dominate local news coverage from Washington. By the next election day, almost every potential voter can identify the names of and rate most House members; only about a half can identify the challengers'. Moreover, the incumbents are more than just empty names: most tend to be well liked and trusted, even by voters who do not share the incumbents' policy preferences.[19] As a result, the incumbents end up as beneficiaries of the lion's share of split ticket, cross-party voting at the congressional level. No wonder more than 90 per cent of the House members who seek reelection win.[20]

This is not to argue that issues have become irrelevant to campaigning. Recent research shows that voters do apparently exercise some retrospective judgment as they cast their ballots for Congress. The electorate regularly uses its opinion about the party in control of the White House (selectively, with great variation across congressional districts) against incumbents identified with national policies of which the electorate disapproves. In some years, the voters are fairly precise in their targets. Strongly pro-Nixon Republicans on the House Judiciary Committee suffered more than the average Republican in 1974, for example. In other years, the targeting is far less exact. In most years and in most districts, though, the voters' judgments about policy—which tend to be judgments about the President and not about the member of Congress's own performance as a legislator— seem not to weigh as heavily as their positive assessments of the incumbents as people.[21]

This kind of retrospective judgment is a far cry from what Federalists and Anti-Federalists were debating in 1787. One crucial reason here, as with so much of what has changed about Congress, is the expanded federal agenda. No one ever thought most voters would devote the time, or have the perspective and inclination, to make a fair assessment of all aspects of a representative's performance. That was why, after all, the framers thought there had to be incentives for members to concentrate on matters their own constituents might not reward.

But the framers did think voters would judge how a representative's decisions about national policy affected the voters' own immediate interests. Even this sometimes seems too much to ask today. Most of the members' serious legislative work is too complicated to be portrayed in the quick news quotes or thirty second television ads that are the staples of modern campaign communication. Instead, campaigns concentrate on raising their candidates' name recognition, identifying swing voter blocs, and mobilizing supporters to turn out. When issues are used, they tend to be ones that raise the swing voters' passions, whether they match the bulk of Congress's business or not.

The incumbent's record may come into the campaign, but usually as a "character" issue (attendance record, junkets, undue influence, etc.), as a snapshot of the incumbent's votes on selected roll call votes, or as a charge raised about one of the few other aspects of an incumbent's work that an interest group or opposition research staff can examine with a computerized data base. Representative X will be described in painfully oversimplified terms as being for or against (or flipflopping on) the elderly, economic growth, runaway spending, dictators, national defense, and so forth. The incumbent may reply that this or that vote was taken out of context. If it was, the reply probably will be futile. The parliamentary context usually is too complicated for anyone but a legislative junkie to understand. The only safe defense for the incumbent, therefore, is to cast every vote with its possible future campaign use in mind. Thus, issues may not be irrelevant to campaigning, but it would be farcical to describe their use as if they involved the informed, sober, second thoughts that the framers wanted from a two-year term.

Mentioning interest groups brings to mind one final way the two-year cycle has changed with the expanded national agenda. The original idea was that two year House and six year Senate terms would permit members to spend time living in the capital city, building a sense of common identity and purpose that would further their deliberations in a setting removed from the immediate pressures of their constituents.

All this has been changed by the growth of national interest groups in Washington. This growth has directly parallelled, and is in some ways another consequence of, the growth of the government's agenda. The first umbrella groups for business and labor grew with the nationalization of the economy and the first major stirrings of national economic regulation at the end of the nineteenth century. The regulatory growth spurt of the Progressive era (roughly 1906–14) was followed, shortly after the end of World War I, by the first Washington lawyer-lobbying firm. The New Deal brought a growth of lawyer-lobbying and an expanded presence by umbrella groups for business, labor and agriculture. The Great Society spurred new forms of "public interest" and clientele representation. Finally, the health, safety, environmental and civil rights laws and regulations of the mid1960s through early 1970s—combined with court decisions and regulations that nationalized a host of "life-style" social issues—increased the importance of Washington to just about everybody. The result was an explosion of interest group representation in the nation's capital.[22]

Interest groups do play important and useful roles for an expanded government, of course. One reason deliberation could not be a solitary activity, it will be remembered, was that discussion helps members become aware of what other districts need. Members need help with the expanded agenda to see how people think they will be affected by legislative proposals. Interest groups also act as important links between Washington and the voters, especially since the 1974 campaign finance law stimulated political action committees (or PACs). But whatever positive benefits interest groups may bring, the one thing they clearly do not do is make Washington a city where the members can deliberate with some sense of distance or insulation.

So the first two items on our list of six—the length of congressional terms and the scope of the national agenda—seem to interact nowadays to intensify particularistic pressures instead of to promote deliberation. Skipping over the third and fourth items, the size of congressional districts and size of the legislature, we come to the way members of Congress advance from one office to the next. Here too, the picture looks very different from 200 years ago. The direct election and nomination of Senators, and the all-but-direct election and nomination of Presidents, has removed peer review as an immediate strategic consideration for politicians who want to advance from one federal office to another. For all practical purposes, candidates can now make direct appeals to the electorate with little or no reference to how effectively they performed in their previous office. The Democratic Party rules that gave office holders seats as unpledged delegates to the 1984 national nominating convention may change this situation slightly. Senator Robert Dole (R– Kansas) might also have changed it slightly if he had been able to defy recent history by turning a party leadership position into an effective launching pad for the presidency in 1988. Even with such changes, however, the basic direction of the past two hundred years has been away from peer review and toward selection by the people. The obvious implication is that politicians who want to move up have to worry more about pleasing primary voters (or potential contributors, volunteers and other supporters,) and less about impressing colleagues with the quality of their work as legislators.

One Countervailing Pressure Favoring Deliberation

So where does that leave Congress? Everything we have said so far would lead one to think everyone spends all of his time worrying only about short-term constituent pressures. Many members do spend a great deal of time on this, of course. But what is truly remarkable is that a relatively fair number of members, and an even higher percentage of the ones who really wield power, seem to have bigger motivations.

The framers seem clearly to have been correct in thinking that a powerful national government would attract a capable group of representatives to Congress. In the nineteenth century, the growth of the government's agenda and the growth of congressional careers went hand in hand.[23] In recent years, the dispersion of power within Congress, combined with the continued growth of the agenda, seems to have cut down sharply the number of members who want to serve in

Congress solely for the pay check, and who do nothing more with the job than to perpetuate themselves in office. Although it would take empirical research to prove the point, it appears that because junior members can exercise power more quickly today, candidates with larger ambitions are gradually replacing Congress's least able members.

This is not meant to portray the new members as self-denying ascetics. The members use the perquisites of office, and they act to preserve their own jobs. But the job is not seen as an end in itself. The members today do not seek the office, and put up with its increasingly straining demands, solely because they are looking for cushy positions. The ones who concentrate on serving their constituents seem genuinely to enjoy that part of their job and consider it important. For others, probably an increasing number, the job is worthwhile because it gives them a chance to exercise power over some portion of federal policy. These latter members build the electoral advantages of incumbency as a way to buy the freedom to pursue other goals in office.

If the members did not care about power and policy, they would be more willing to let others exercise power in their names. The increased prominence of floor amendments and collegial party meetings, and the concomitant decline in the deference members pay to committee expertise (shown in recent research by The Brookings Institution's Steven Smith,[24]) are signs of the importance today's members place on not being read out of key policy decisions. Fractionalization, therefore, seems to be both a cause and an effect of having members who care about results: a cause for the way decentralized power influences the career decisions of potential candidates; an effect for the aggressively active way the new members insist on using the power the post-reform Congress gives them.

It is remarkable how many members—and especially, how many chairmen—use their positions to raise tough issues it would be easier to avoid. Some members might be inclined by their own characters to raise such issues as soon as they have the institutional power to do so—whether because they seek national fame, want to be considered important among insiders, or feel a straightforward concern for the nation's welfare. Even more interesting from the perspective of institutional incentives, however, is to see chairmen or party leaders pushed by their own followers' expectations. Martha Derthick and Paul Quirk present a fascinating picture in *The Politics of Deregulation* of former Senator Howard Cannon, then chairman of the Commerce Committee, deciding to work on an issue he previously had ignored because his committee felt embarrassed when another one gained credit for promoting airline deregulation. The Commerce Committee had jurisdiction over the subject, and committee members all had a stake in acting like "statesmen" if they wanted to preserve their own committee's turf and reputation.[25] In the 99th Congress (1985–86), many of the actions taken on tax reform by Dan Rostenkowski (House Ways and Means Committee) and Robert Packwood (Senate Finance Committee) can also be explained by the two chairmen's desire to enhance their own reputations and power within their respective chambers.

It may well be true that party leaders have fewer levers in the post–1970s reform period for persuading followers to behave in a statesmanlike way. Nevertheless, the followers' own expectations still create incentives for those party, committee, subcommittee and *ad hoc* coalition leaders who want to enhance their reputations and power, to raise issues that force Congress to behave like something more than an instantaneous reflection of immediate constituencies. What is at work here, it seems, is a kind of a self-selection process that gets us to the final point the framers talked about: how members wield power within the institution. If a member of Congress wants to get something accomplished—not if he wants to block somebody else's project, but if he wants to get something positive through the legislative labyrinth—the member cannot hope to get anywhere unless he has developed the respect and trust of his colleagues. Members who want to exercise power have to gain that respect. Yes, a member can become a committee or subcommittee chairman without earning his colleagues' respect first. But the chairman cannot accomplish very much unless he first earns the support of his committee and then a majority of the full chamber.

This is not to say that Congress is just as it was in 1789. Since 1910, and especially since the early 1970s, the pressures from outside the institution have increased, while the inside rewards and sanctions available to party and committee leaders have been cut back. The internal incentives the framers cared about are weaker today than two decades ago. But, despite all this change, the members have been able to avoid always giving in to immediate pressures. There seem to be three different reasons for this. (1) First, most of the members are able to make their own seats fairly safe for reelection. That gives them more freedom to pursue their own broad policy objectives. (2) Second, freedom does not mean very much unless you want to do something with it. Most of the members really do care about issues broader than their own survival. If anything, there seem to be more members with broad policy interests in Congress today than there used to be. (3) Finally, the people who are most likely to wield power within Congress are forced by the very desire to wield power to adopt a broad, national perspective on policy.

Those are three good reasons why Congress still is able to break out of parochial blindness on many occasions. But that does not, to repeat, mean that the world is unchanged. Today's congressional leaders may be people who care about national issues, but leaders have to work within the context set by the followers. If the followers feel more pressed by outside forces than they once did, you can rest assured that those pressures will also be felt by the leadership. The members today do feel a great deal of pressure from their constituents. They always will and should feel this in a democracy, but the level of pressure has probably gone up. The internal incentive structure still helps to balance those pressures, but the rewards leaders can use to buttress the internal incentive structures have been weakened. Right now, the situation may seem more or less in balance. But what can we expect in the foreseeable future?

Looking Ahead

It would be absurd to try to predict all the major ways Congress will change in the coming century. I shall pick a more manageable question: how will changes in communications technology over the next few decades be likely to affect the internal incentives *in*, and external pressures *on*, the legislative branch? Because space is limited and the issue speculative, my answer will have to be sketchy.

The basic outlines of the communications/technological revolution of the past decade are well known. Computers have made it possible to perform sophisticated information storage, retrieval and manipulation tasks that were not possible a few decades ago, at a cost unimaginable only ten years also. At the same time, "narrowcasting" through radio, cable television, and low power television is making inroads on network broadcasting. Finally, interactive communication has made instant mass surveys on pending legislation a realistic vision. Technology makes it possible to imagine members of Congress, or interest groups, posing a question in the morning and getting a mass response by the afternoon, in time for a vote.

We cannot predict the next decade's technology. However, we can begin thinking about how change might affect the legislative process. In a recent draft manuscript, F. Christopher Arterton of Harvard's Kennedy Institute of Politics suggested that we look at the vast array of new technologies in terms of the way they affect (1) the flow of communication between members and constituents and (2) the flow between interest groups and Congress.[26]

Technology probably has helped, and will continue to help, the member much more than the constituent. The individual, unaffiliated constituent still writes letters one at a time, but once the letter comes in, the member can put the constituent's name in a sophisticated data base and churn out targeted mailings forever. This is not likely to change, because constituents cannot pay for the technology and members can. That means that technology will help the member win reelection and thus continue to help buy the member freedom for action.

What about interest groups? The communications revolution has made it possible for many small to medium sized groups to follow Congress without hiring large staffs. For $30,000—the cost of one researcher—a group can now can get complete online documentary databases with instant search capabilities. Without the computer, no staff (no matter how large) could duplicate this capability.

What is the effect of this interest group technology on the legislative process? Two kinds of activities can be distinguished. It was argued earlier that groups can contribute important information to the deliberative process in a complex government. Technology helps this along. But everyone knows groups do not exist just to communicate substantive information. The same technical capability that helps groups analyze substance, also helps them get their members to exert pressure on Congress quickly. "Just push a button", said William Miller, president of Miller Legislative Services to *The Washington Post*, "and you've sent a letter to your entire congressional district."[27]

What difference does that make? Remember that the Constitution's framers wanted to give Congress some sense of distance from local constituency pressures. The new interest group communication technology promises to all but wipe out this sense of distance. In time, this could become a serious threat to the Framer's design. It would be silly, however, to respond by prohibiting new communication technologies or interest groups. That is precisely the approach James Madison rejected in *Federalist* 10. If Congress wants to respond in a meaningful way, it will have to buttress its own internal devices for rewarding members who choose to resist.

Over the past decade, Congress weakened a whole range of institutional incentives and then ended up relying on the members' residual, personal concern for the national interest. That will not be enough for the future. The country has been relying on an implausible combination of Federalist and Anti-Federalist positions. The Federalists thought concern for the national interest was too weak a reed upon which to build institutional incentives; Anti-Federalists thought you can and should build on civic virtue, but only in a small, simple republic. We now have a complex, multifactional, Federalist-style republic that may be getting by on a misplaced and excessive Anti-Federalist-style reliance on the civic virtue of people in office. If the country's need for a deliberative legislative process is going to withstand the inevitable pressures new technology will bring to the system, it must, to paraphrase Madison, think about Federalist solutions to the Federalist problems of innovation and complexity. That brings us, finally, to the subject of reform.

Constitutional Reform?

Constitutional reform is a favorite topic, naturally enough, in this bicentennial year. It is important in light of the previous analysis to point out that the most popular and most highly publicized strand of contemporary reformist thought tries to address the problem raised here by giving the President more power over Congress, and by strengthening the political parties within Congress.[28]

These reformist ideas are attractive, but they appear to have serious problems. Underlying these proposals are assumptions that would tie the self-interest of Members of Congress to that of their President through more disciplined political parties. But to produce disciplined, democratic parties, there are only two possibilities: one is a disciplined multi-party system and the other is a disciplined two-party system.

A multi-party system is a much more likely possibility than two disciplined parties in the United States, given the country's post-Federalist diversity. Such a multi-party system would simply move bargaining away from Congress to another collective body, a cabinet or a legislative steering committee. But the examples of multi-party parliamentary governments the world over make it doubtful that this would produce a government better able to deliberate, better able to resist pressure, or better able to act in the national interest, than the one we now have.

The other possibility is a disciplined two-party system. But the two-party discipline presupposes either a country much less diverse than the United States, or one that has become polarized by deeply divisive issues. To repeat that point; the only way to get a disciplined, two-party system in the United States would be by polarizing the population around divisive issues first. The cost of two party discipline, in other words, would mean endangering the most fundamental of all the constitutional decisions taken in 1787: the decision to encourage diversity as part of an effort to preserve liberty, and to make politics less a life and death matter than it can be in small republics.

Many of the Constitution's critics, impatient with what they see as stalemate, maintain that our two hundred year old document has produced a hopelessly inefficient government. Efficiency is a word that has little content, however, apart from the ends one is trying to achieve. A process that resolves disputes quickly may not be an efficient way to assure that policies have popular support, or will pursue agreed upon ends. Discipline may be efficient for some objectives, but far less efficient for others. Collective deliberation may well be the *most efficient* way to serve the ends of a liberal, democratic-republican, representative self-government for most broad issues of legislative policy.

It turns out that the institutions the framers designed are well matched to the Constitution's most fundamental purpose of avoiding polarization and civil war. If that purpose remains desirable, it means that Congress's response to the challenges of technology and complexity should be more modest than what the constitutional reformers are proposing. The average Member of Congress is not likely to support recentralizing the power that was decentralized in the 1970s. So, future Congresses should aim to buttress the various *collegial* mechanisms that create incentives for cooperation, without trying to make the mechanisms directly coercive. The congressional budget process has been a useful tool for increasing cooperation in a subject filled with tough choices. The congressional party's election committees have also played important roles here, with their increased electoral importance and with their issue-based generic advertising. I recommend a series of campaign finance reforms that would make congressional parties even more important and powerful in the election process. Other proposals might look at committee assignments, floor access, or a host of other ways of strengthening the forces that take a national perspective. The important point, though, is that all of these changes involve statutes and congressional rules of procedure. The Constitution does not need a fundamental change to meet the challenge of the republic's third century.

Endnotes

1. Max Farrand, ed. *The Records of the Federal Convention of 1787* (New Haven: Yale University Press, 1937) in 4 volumes, Vol. II, p. 638. Hereafter cited as Farrand.

2. Alexander Hamilton, James Madison and John Jay, *The Federalist*, Jacob E. Cooke, ed. (Middletown, Conn.: Wesleyan University Press, 1961), *Federalist* No. 10, p. 58.

3. See Gordon Wood, *The Creation of the American Republic, 1776–1787* (New York: Norton, 1972), pp. 53–70.

4. *Federalist* No. 10, p. 58.

5. *Federalist* No. 10, p. 60.

6. *Federalist* No. 51, p. 349.

7. Jack N. Rakove, *The Beginnings of National Politics: An Interpretive History of the Continental Congress* (Baltimore: John Hopkins University Press, 1979), p. 233.

8. Jonathan Elliot, ed. *The Debates of the Several State Conventions on the Adoption of the Federal Constitution As Recommended by the General Convention at Philadelphia in 1787*, 5 volumes, 2d edition, (New York, 1888), Vol. II, p. 306. Hereafter cited as Elliot.

9. Elliot, II, 10–11.

10. Elliott, II, 4.

11. Farrand, II, 198.

12. Elliot, III, 30.

13. *Federalist* No. 55, p. 374.

14. *Ibid.*, p. 375. See also Hamilton in Elliot, II, 349.

15. *Federalist* No. 55, p. 374.

16. Elliot, IV, 286.

17. Joseph Martin as told to Robert Donovan, *My First Fifty Years in Politics* (New York: McGraw-Hill, 1960), p. 49; quoted in Nelson Polsby, "The Washington Community, 1960–1980," in T. Mann and N. Ornstein, eds. *The New Congress* (Washington: American Enterprise Institute, 1981), p. 30.

18. This is a conservative estimate that counts only what the average member spends on personal staff based in the district, other office expenses spent in the district, a small percentage of the budget for the Washington office staff, and the value of free postage for mail that is initiated by the office. It does not count mail sent as a direct response to a letter from someone else, the value of free radio and television studios provided by the congressional parties, or other important benefits whose value is hard to quantify from readily available data. See N. Ornstein, T. Mann, M. Malbin, A. Schick and J. Bibby, *Vital Statistics on Congress, 1984–1985 Edition* (Washington: American Enterprise Institute, 1984), pp. 123, 131–34.

19. See, for example, Thomas E. Mann and Raymond E. Wolfinger, "Candidates and Parties in Congressional Elections," *American Political Science Review*, 74:617–32 (Sept. 1980).

20. N. Ornstein, *et al.*, *Vital Statistics*, pp. 49–50. 21. See Gary C. Jacobson, *The Politics of Congressional elections*, 2d ed., (Boston: Little, Brown, 1987), pp. 140–48 and the sources there cited.

22. See Michael J. Malbin, "Looking Back at the Future of Campaign Finance Reform," in M. Malbin, ed. *Money and Politics in the United States: Financing Elections in the 1980s* (Chatham, NJ: American Enterprise Institute and Chatham House, 1984), pp. 249–50.

23. Samuel J. Kernell, "Toward Understanding 19th Century Congressional Careers: Ambition, Competition and Rotation," *American Journal of Political Science*, 21:669–93 (1977). Kernell argues that congressional careers became longer in part because the office was seen as being more attractive. The assertion that part of the increased attractiveness stemmed from the growing role of the national government is my own.

24. Steven Smith, "Revolution in the House: Let's Do It on the Floor," Discussion Papers in Governmental Studies, No. 5 (Washington, D.C.: The Brookings Institution, 1986).

25. Martha Derthick and Paul Quirk, *The Politics of Deregulation* (Washington, D.C.: Brookings, 1986), pp. 108–11.

26. F. Christopher Arterton, "Democratic Representation: An Examination of Issues Created by New Communication Technology in the Context of the Constitutional Bicentennial," draft manuscript, 1987.

27. Mark Lawrence, "Computers Generate The On-Line Lobbyist," *The Washington Post*, June 26, 1987, p. A23.

28. See, for example, Donald L. Robinson, ed., *Reforming American Government: The Bicentennial Papers of the Committee on the Constitutional System* (Boulder, Colo.: Westview Press, 1985) and James Sundquist *Constitutional Reform and Effective Government* (Washington, D.C.: Brookings, 1986).

The Changing
Nature of the Presidency

Dorothy Buckton James
Dean, School of Government and Public Administration
The American University.

The Constitution of the United States is not simply about organization or structure. It is profoundly concerned with human nature. It is philosophically opposed to the concept of human nature articulated in the Declaration of Independence. Consequently, the organization it establishes to govern humans differs markedly from that of the Articles of Confederation, which applied the Declaration's philosophy to governance.

One of our particular triumphs as Americans has been to obscure those differences so effectively from ourselves that we can speak warmly of the "Founding Fathers," unselfconsciously lumping together individuals who anathematized each other's philosophies. A brief comparison of the documents clarifies the point.

Human Rationality: The Democratic Philosophy of The Declaration

The second paragraph of the Declaration of Independence is a succinct summary of John Locke's philosophy:

> We hold these truths to be self-evident, that all men are created equal; that they are endowed by their Creator with certain inalienable rights; that among these, are life, liberty, and the pursuit of happiness. That, to secure these rights, governments are instituted among men, deriving their just powers from the consent of the governed; . . .

This rationalistic vision of a metaphysical entity establishing rules for human conduct that can be known through human reason and can be the basis for government accountability was articulated in the Declaration in 1776 and given structural application to human governance in the Articles of Confederation, submitted in 1777 and ratified in 1781. There was significant overlap between the signers of the two documents.[1]

Few Americans have any familiarity with the Articles. Most of those who are even aware of them tend to describe them as a first, immature attempt at governance from which we learned enough to develop the effective document, with which we have lived for two hundred years. However functional this myth may be in obscuring fundamental differences among the Founding Fathers, it is absurd. The minds of those who drafted the Declaration and Articles were hardly inferior to those of the Federalists. The difference was philosophic.

If one views humans as rational, equal and endowed with inalienable rights whose protection is the purpose of government, then democracy is the only tolerable form of government. Like Rousseau later, the authors of the Articles considered it necessary to protect against abuse of government power by decentralization, retaining control at the local level. National government was an unavoidable necessity for the reasons that have been the basis of all national governments—the need to maintain internal order (particularly economic) and to protect against external aggression (English, Spanish, French and Indians). The Articles' structure was that of all governments where unity is considered necessary but the constituent units fear control from the center and attempt to limit any exercise of power (e.g., the League of Nations or the United Nations).

It was styled as a "firm league of friendship" in which each state retained its sovereignty, freedom, and independence. It established a unicameral Congress whose delegates were annually appointed in such manner as each state legislature should decide and could be recalled at any time. Each state had one vote. Taxes and military manpower were handled by a quota system paid by each state. No separation of powers was necessary, since power itself was intended to be so limited. Thus limited judicial functions were exercised by Congress as a whole in the event that states were involved in a mutual dispute. No executive power, as we use the term, was provided.

In short, the weak governmental structure established by the Articles of Confederation was a necessary and appropriate form of organization for those with the philosophy of rational, perfectible human beings expressed in the Declaration of Independence. It could not possibly have been amended by the 1787 convention, whatever the pretext under which that gathering had been called to remedy the Articles' defects. Its democratic philosophy was unacceptable to Federalists, who organized the conservative counter-revolution. That convention included only eight individuals who had been associated with the earlier documents.[2] The remaining thirty-one delegates included major figures whose philosophy gave short shrift to rationalistic concepts of human nature: George Washington, Alexander Hamilton, James Madison, and Rufus King.

Human Factionalism: The Republican
Philosophy of The Constitution

Just as the Declaration expressed the philosophy that found structural embodiment in the Articles, so *The Federalist Papers* expressed the philosophy that found structural embodiment in the Constitution. *The Federalist Papers*, a collection of newspaper articles written by Madison, Hamilton and Jay, designed to convince New Yorkers to ratify the Constitution, many stand as one of the world's most elegant examples of political propaganda. James Madison succinctly expressed its philosophy in *Federalist* 10. In contrast to Jefferson's democratic vision, Madison found mankind to be selfish, short-sighted, and inherently given to faction.

> . . . By a faction, I understand a number of citizens, whether amounting to a majority or minority of the whole, who are united and actuated by some common impulse of passion, or of interest, adverse to the rights of other citizens, or to the permanent and aggregate interests of the community. . . . As long as the reason of man continues fallible, and he is at liberty to exercise it, different opinions will be formed. As long as the connection subsists between his reason and his self-love, his opinions and his passions will have a reciprocal influence on each other; . . . The latent causes of faction are thus sown in the nature of man; . . . the most common and durable source of factions has been the various and unequal distribution of property . . . . the causes of faction cannot be removed; and . . . relief is only to be sought in the means of controlling its effects.

It is to control the effects of these inherent imperfections in human nature to which the Constitution was addressed. *Federalist* 10 began with the statement that "Among the numerous advantages promised by a well constructed Union, none deserves to be more accurately developed than its tendency to break and control the violence of faction." Federalists found democracy inherently subject to the "mischiefs of faction," incompatible with personal security or the rights of property. In a thinly veiled attack on Jefferson's enthusiasm for democracy, Madison wrote:

> Theoretical politicians, who have patronized this species of government have erroneously supposed, that by reducing mankind to a perfect equality in their political rights! they would, at the same time, be perfectly equalized and assimilated in their possessions, their opinions, and their passions.

The Federalist solution to the ills of democracy was the introduction of what they called "republican" principles which entailed "delegation of the government to a small number of citizens elected by the rest," and extension of that government to a larger number of citizens and territory in order to dilute the impact of factions.

In this "compound republic" Madison stated that the people would surrender much of their power to a central government. To guard against usurpation that power was divided between two distinct levels of government (national and state) and in each level subdivided among distinct and separate departments (executive, bicameral legislature and judiciary). Hence, in the words of *Federalist* 51:

> . . . a double security arises to the rights of the people. The different governments will control each other; at the same time that each will be controlled by itself.

A simple, weak central government was necessary to protect the people under Jefferson's democratic theory, whereas republican principles necessitated a complex structure. Two concepts that are anathema to democratic theorists, "control" and "power," were essential if humanity is characterized not by the warmly emotive noun "The People," but by the negative one, "Faction." When that aristocratic Virginian, James Madison, referred to him, "the common man" clearly lacked dentifrice, deodorant and education.

In *Federalist* 51, Madison enthusiastically took aim at the Achilles heel of Lockian/Jeffersonian rationalism: if humans have sufficient reason to know their Creator's will, why do they not follow it without the coercion inherent in even the mildest form of government?

> . . . what is government itself, but the greatest of all reflections on human nature? If men were angels, no government would be necessary. If angels were to govern men, neither external nor internal controls on government would be necessary. In framing a government, which is to be administered by men over men, the great difficulty lies in this: You must first enable the government to control the governed; and in the next place, oblige it to control itself. A dependence on the people is, no doubt, the primary control on the government; but experience has taught mankind the necessity of auxiliary precautions.

Those "auxiliary precautions" are the whole system of separate institutions given different constituencies and terms that provides the necessary *motives* to check each other, and the elaborate check and balance system that provides the necessary *means* to oblige the government to control itself.

The office of President was an essential part of this structure. There was no similar need for executive power under the democratic philosophy of the Articles, but the Constitution's republican principles assumed the necessity of a strong exercise of executive power, safeguarded by the check and balance system.

The Presidency: Integral to Federalist Philosophy

Alexander Hamilton actively defended the office of President against charges by democrats that it smacked of the return of kingship. In *Federalist* 70 he noted that:

> . . . Energy in the executive is a leading character in the definition of good government. It is essential to the protection of the community against foreign attacks. It is not less essential to the steady administration of the laws, to the protection of property against those irregular and high-handed combinations, which sometimes interrupt the ordinary course of justice, to the security of liberty against the enterprises and assaults of ambition, of faction and of anarchy. . . A feeble executive implies a feeble execution of the government. A feeble execution is but another phrase for a bad execution: and a government ill executed, whatever it may be in theory, must be, in practice, a bad government. . The ingredients which constitute energy in the executive are, unity; duration; and adequate provision for its support; competent powers.

Federalists believed that the energy they vested in a President was limited by the check and balance system exercised by the other branches, particularly Congress, and by:

> . . . the election of the president once in four years by persons immediately chosen by the people for that purpose; his liability, at all times, to impeachment, trial, dismission from office, incapacity to serve in any other, and to the forfeiture of life and estate by subsequent prosecution in the common course of Law.[3]

With that much control of the government, Federalists felt comfortable in writing Article II creating an executive office unique in human experience. The power of that office is supported by three pillars, its roles as Commander-in-Chief, Chief-of-State, and Chief Executive of national government programs. Through two hundred years, presidential power has rested on those three pillars. Thus, whenever Americans list or speak of "powerful" presidents they are referring to men in whose terms one or more of those three pillars of Presidential power held major significance for the nation.

For example, George Washington, Thomas Jefferson, Andrew Jackson, and Theodore Roosevelt are often designated as "powerful" presidents for the significance during their terms of national programs that enhanced their stature in the role of Chief Executive. As President, Washington established the national departments and developed the whole system of national administration. Jefferson engaged in initiatives such as the Louisiana Purchase. Jackson's involvement with administering national programs for internal improvements and his well publicized battle with the banks enhanced his image as a leader. Similarly, Teddy Roosevelt's efforts in conservation exemplified the significance of the role of Chief Executive as a pillar of presidential power.

Other Presidents who are customarily considered to have been "strong" derived their power from the Commander in Chief and/or Chief of State roles. Thus Abraham Lincoln and Woodrow Wilson are always included in lists of major presidents for their use of presidential power in the Civil and First World Wars, respectively.

What characterizes the contemporary presidency is the fact that since Franklin Delano Roosevelt's day all three aspects of presidential power have become continuous, daily issues of concern for American government. Consequently, the visibility and significance of the presidency has been enhanced. Since the Second World War, the United States has been a world power for whom foreign policy has been a daily national concern, enhancing the President's role as Chief-of-State. Similarly, in a world of cold war and "limited" wars, the United States could never again declare that it had made the world safe for democracy and return to private interests. To the degree that military policy has become a daily national concern (increasingly inseparable from foreign policy), the president's role as Commander-in-Chief has been enhanced. Finally, beginning with FDR and accelerating since then, especially since John Fitzgerald Kennedy's day, major national programs have proliferated, inevitably enhancing presidential visibility as Chief Executive.

The result of the enhancement of these three major pillars has been perceived as the growth of presidential power. Virtually all presidents from FDR to Ronald Reagan are viewed as "strong": Franklin Roosevelt, Truman, Eisenhower, Kennedy, Johnson, Nixon and Reagan. Ford and Carter are not usually included in such lists but we may be too close to their Presidencies to judge effectively. Time will provide historical perspective to balance contemporary negative assessments.

This enhancement of the three pillars of presidential power has received much public attention. It has often been discussed in terms of a shift of power toward the President, often derided as unbalancing the check and balance system intended by the Federalists to protect against usurpation.

To assess the degree to which the check and balance system has been eroded, it is useful to consider the nature of power as exercised by the executive and legislative branches.

"Active" vs. "Negative" Power: The Gap Between Initiative and Implementation

Those who write of the shift of power toward the President often express a highly simplistic concept of the nature of power. In fact, most Americans seem to think of power solely in its "active" side. When asked to define it, Americans will say things like, power is:

- getting things done, getting what you want
- setting your own agenda
- persuading or influencing others
- control

Underlying these phrases is a vision of governmental power as being an active force in which an individual can *initiate* policies that he or she desires. That is indeed power, but it is only one of its two delicious flavors. (Power is always delicious to those who exercise it.) The other side of power is the "negative" capacity to block, delay, prevent, change, dilute and otherwise alter the initiatives of others. In short, active power is the ability to initiate policies you wish to achieve, whereas negative power is the ability to prevent the implementation of such initiatives by others.

Until the 1930s, the primary locus of the active power to initiate policy lay with Congress, only shifting to the President during those brief periods when one or more of the three pillars of presidential power was prominent, such as in the Presidencies of Jackson, Lincoln or Wilson. Afterward, however, it returned to Congressional hands. Thus, for example, between the Presidencies of Lincoln and Wilson, with a few notable exceptions, such as Cleveland or Teddy Roosevelt, there was a string of Presidents sufficiently undistinguished that most Americans today would be hard pressed to name them. Active power in the Gilded Age was held by Congress, particularly the Senate.

What characterizes the contemporary presidency is the inevitable and irreversible shift of active, initiating power to the executive branch. The shift has occurred, as discussed earlier, because mid- to late twentieth century America is committed to daily prominent involvement in issues of foreign and military policy and to the administration of broad national programs. Given his roles as Commander in Chief, Chief of State and Chief Executive, primary responsibility for initiating public policy has shifted to the President. He is responsible for initiating the legislative agenda, sending draft bills to Congress across the broad range of policy issues facing the nation. That is not to say that some bills are not still initiated in the legislature, but the *primary* responsibility for policy initiative in our system has clearly shifted to the executive branch. With it has come the institutionalization of the Presidency from an elected official assisted by a few immediate advisors and secretaries to the Executive Office of the President with councils on a range of topics from national security to economic policy, with public relations staff, legislative liaison, and staff to manage and orchestrate the relations between these proliferating institutions and staff, and their access to the President.

This shift since FDR's day of active, initiating power to the President has been widely noted and often bewailed as causing an imbalance in the system of checks and balances intended by the Constitution. Much of this discussion seems irrelevant, however, as it is based on an erroneous assumption that power is a zero-sum game. If the Presidency is getting "stronger" then it is assumed that Congress must be getting "weaker."

Reports of Congress's demise, however, have been greatly exaggerated. While responsibility for initiating public policy has indeed shifted toward the President, Congress has not gracefully bowed out of the power struggle. The Federalists designed their structure too well for that. They recognized that:

> . . . the great security against a gradual concentration of the several powers in the same department, consists in giving to those who administer each department, the necessary constitutional means, and personal motives, to resist encroachments of the others. The provision for defense must in this, as in all other cases, be made commensurate to the danger of attack. Ambition must be made to counteract ambition. The interest of the man must be connected with the constitutional rights of the place.[4]

Ambition has indeed been made to counteract ambition. As the active power of initiation has moved to the President, Congress has increasingly developed its negative powers. The result has been a growing gap between initiative and implementation in our system. The President increasingly finds himself blustering like Shakespeare's Glendower that: "I can call spirits from the vastly deep," only to be plagued by Hotspur's eternal question: "Why so can I, or so can any man, but will they come when you do call for them?"[5]

The Growing Gap Between Initiative and Implementation

The period of the 1960s was marked by frequent stalemates between the two branches. In fact, Kennedy's actual legislative record was fairly weak. Few key pieces of his proposed legislation passed Congress during his lifetime. The difficulties were obscured by the early Johnson years in which his own exceptional legislative skill, his ability to capitalize on post-assassination support for Kennedy's legislative agenda, and his own initiatives, especially after the 1964 landslide election, enabled him to achieve a passage rate on his legislative initiatives that rivaled Roosevelt's in the early New Deal days. That success rate diminished as he became increasingly mired in

Vietnam. Certainly his three successors experienced the frustration of legislative stalemate.

Beyond the normal means written into the Constitution to assure conflict between the executive and legislative branches, during the 1970s Congress underwent a broad range of internal changes that created the "New Congress" which is better positioned to mount a more determined and effective resistance to the President than ever before. In short, while the President's active power of initiative was increasing, Congress developed equally potent tools of negative power to check and balance the Executive branch.

Prior to 1970, Congress was a collection of dispersed concentrations of power held by chairmen of the standing committees. The chairman's preeminent power was based on procedures, secrecy, information and the manner in which the federal budget was constructed. Congressional procedures enhanced chairmen's power in many ways: they could "pigeonhole" bills; they appointed subcommittee members and chairmen; they controlled the agenda, including all points of order in discussing a bill within committee; they could call meetings during a period of legislative recess or when members were not generally available, and collect proxy votes from their friends on the committee; influenced by a chairman's request, the House Rules Committee could vote to have the House consider a bill on a "closed" rule to protect it as it came from committee, or an "open" one. Committee meetings were closed not only to the public, but also to other members of Congress and the Congressional staffs, providing chairmen with the power of secrecy. Their careful control of the flow of information made individual members dependent on those who held the information, who could, in turn, exact promises of support for information. The federal budget was dealt with piecemeal in various appropriations subcommittees with the full Appropriations Committee generally rubber-stamping what the subcommittees decided. Lacking any overall review, those who had their hands on the bits and pieces of the budget (chairmen of the committees and subcommittees) could use it to their advantage, and did.

This system was supported by the seniority system of automatic accession to chairmanships.[6] Technically there were procedures for removing chairmen but they were never used. Realistically, no one had the power to depose chairmen. Thus they were not accountable to other members.

There was no assured countervailing power to committee chairmen. Party leaders (majority and minority leaders or the Speaker of the House) were generally inactive, ineffective, and unaggressive (e.g., McCormack or Mansfield) and were not given much power by the rules. Those party leaders who exercised more control (e.g., Sam Rayburn or Lyndon Johnson) had built their position by the sheer force of their personalities and their personal drive. It was not institutionalized in the rules. Members had even less power than party leaders.

The implications of this organizational structure for the President are clear. While legislative power was decentralized, there were a limited number of individuals who held it. Negotiations could be held with the relevant chairman or chairmen and if a bargain could be struck a President could be assured that they could deliver. The process of influence and negotiation was difficult, but defined.

The Legislative Reorganization Act of 1970 and changes accelerating since then have created the "New Congress" in which power has gravitated from the committee chairmen to the party leaders and in which individual rank and file members have a great deal of flexibility.[7] Most of the power "perks" of chairmen were ended by the Legislative Reorganization Act: they cannot pigeonhole bills; proxy voting is now very restricted; their leeway and leverage over subcommittee membership and chairmanship has been reduced or eliminated; and unless the majority of a committee votes in public and on the record to close them, all meetings are open, so the power of secrecy is gone.

Information now comes from a lot of places for rank and file members. Staffs of Congress (individual and committee/subcommittee staffs) have increased substantially since 1970. Therefore, there is a lot of information available to Congressmen without having to depend on chairmen. Agencies have been created to provide more information to Congress in general and to individual members in particular. For example, the Office of Technology Assessment provides members with studies on the impact of each piece of legislation that has a technological aspect; the Congressional Budget Office provides economic information not previously available to Congressmen. Two old agencies have been upgraded and expanded to provide additional information to members, the Legislative Reference Service and the General Accounting Office. Technology has substantially improved the information flow through computer terminals and services such as "dial-a-bill" that are available to any member or staff person.

While the rules have been changing, so has the budget process. Against Presidential initiatives, the Congressional Budget Act of 1974 provided Congress a tool of far greater centralization and coordination of the budget. There has to be a shared decision on the overall total of allocation to major areas. The requirement of such a Congressional decision diminishes the fragmentation of Congressional decision-making and puts significant restraints on the range of Presidential choices and bargaining.

Seniority has been broken, leading to a three-way split of power in the House, and to a lesser degree in the Senate, between the chairmen, party caucus and party leaders. The President has to deal with all three, not just the chairmen. He must learn what levers are open to him. This demands a more skillful, knowledgeable and diplomatic, more politically sensitive President than was previously necessary.

All of these changes in the 1970s occurred simultaneously with an unprecedented turnover rate in Congress. Thus, the new opportunities for the rank and file occurred at a time when a large new group of legislators were entering the system, who had not been socialized to earlier norms of seniority or to Speaker Sam Rayburn's adage, "to get along, go along." As a result of these changes a President needs far more political sensitivity, more effective Congressional liaison staff, and has less likelihood of achieving his ends through Congress than has been the case in this century.

The Gap Obscured by Reagan's First Term

While the presidencies of Kennedy, Johnson, Nixon, Ford and Carter demonstrate the increasing gap between initiative and implementation, Ronald Reagan's first term appeared to reverse the trend. Reagan was exceptionally successful in achieving the implementation of his initiatives throughout his first term and even into the first two years of his second.

Reagan's presidency, however, does not mark the beginning of a trend toward greater capacity on the part of the President to reduce the gap between initiative and implementation. Rather, it reflects aspects of good fortune and personal skill that are specific to one individual, not transferrable.

In several ways during his first term circumstances conspired to make Ronald Reagan the luckiest of all the contemporary Presidents. First, he was elected in an era when Americans across all regions, classes and factional interests agreed that there was one paramount national issue, inflation, and that the President was the official to take the initiative on that issue. Thus the President's mandate was clear and his preeminent position in setting and carrying out policy to deal with it was acknowledged. A single clear electoral mandate is rare for American presidents unless they face a major cross-cutting issue such as civil war, world war, or the Great Depression. Otherwise, a President is elected by a coalition of votes cast by individuals who divide on the issues for which they chose him. One political scientist described this coalition as a "sticky ball of popcorn."[8] The minute a President acts, some of the kernels flake off because their reason for voting for him either was not relevant to the areas in which he takes action, or was possibly even contrary to the particular action taken. To have a single clear issue and public acceptance of your legitimacy to act is a rare stroke of good luck for a President. It was used skillfully by President Reagan not only as a mandate for action, but as a way to avoid taking action on the divisive social issues that had been the basis of his support by the "Moral Majority." Thus he could assure Jerry Falwell or Strom Thurmond of his support for their views, and his intention to take action to reverse public policies on school prayers, busing, abortion and general moral "permissiveness." Yet he could put off the date of such action until he had dealt with the more pressing issue of inflation. Since that issue was not easily amenable to his solutions, there were several years during which he could claim that it had to be his first priority, supported by a continuing broad mandate in public opinion polls.

A second aspect of Reagan's good fortune was the fact that in his first term no international crisis or domestic scandal unexpectedly rose to put an uncontrollable spin on the ball of presidential initiative. There was no Bay of Pigs which troubled Kennedy, no Vietnam War which sucked Johnson into a quagmire from which he could not extricate himself, no Watergate scandal which destroyed Nixon's Presidency, nor any world crisis over an oil shortage which limited Ford's effectiveness. No incidents occurred like those that enabled the Ayatollah Khomeini to turn President Carter into an international symbol of impotence. There were moments of brinkmanship in Nicaragua or Lebanon, but good fortune and skill always enabled Reagan to beat a strategic retreat in time. No scandals affecting his administration surfaced during the first term in a way that directly involved him.

A third aspect of his good fortune was the collapse of world oil prices. This contributed substantially to the decline in the rate of inflation.

Ironically, a fourth aspect of his good fortune was the timing and impact of the assassination attempt. In writing this there is no intention of making light of that attempt. It is an awe-ful thing to contemplate the assassination of a head of state. The point is that the event enabled Reagan to gain inestimable political capital. It gave the President a unique opportunity early in his Presidency to build personal public support that transcended the normal barriers of partisanship. The best aspects of his personality were clearly projected into every American living room through the medium of television. He was confident, strong, brave, decent, charitable to his assailant, humorous, warm and gracious. He comforted the country in his and its hour of need.

At least as great a benefit as the personal support he gained from public opinion, was the support he gained from legislators and the Washington press corps as a result of the assassination attempt and his effective handling of it. Washington insiders knew how much more serious were his injuries than the public was initially told. Therefore, they could more fully appreciate with what an effort he handled his job in the early months after the attempt. His first act after returning from the hospital to the White House was a speech to reassure the nation. He could easily have made it from the Oval Office, but chose instead to go before a joint session of Congress. Symbolically, this was a strong indication that the government was united and undamaged by the assassination attempt. It also brought him widespread respect from legislators of both parties and from the press who knew the pain it cost. Reinforced by extensive public support, that respect gave him several years of leverage and bought crucial time from criticism by Congress and the press.

For example, the press dropped its normal demands for press conferences and accepted a lower level of competence on the President's part than had been demanded of his predecessors in office. He frequently misspoke himself without occasioning more than the mildest of press comments. Compare press handling of frequently misstated facts during the press conferences of his first term with the intensive way the media emphasized blunders of speech, even those made in the heat of debate, e.g., Ford on Polish democracy, or Nixon on Quemoy and Matsu. When the probing but respectful questions of Sam Donaldson are the worst the press can throw at a President he must count himself fortunate indeed.

Reagan's ability to narrow the gap between initiative and implementation cannot be ascribed merely to luck, or circumstances, important though they have been. He also demonstrated exceptional skill, particularly during his first term, in communicating his initiatives clearly and capitalizing on the high level of personal support to cause those initiatives to be implemented.

As a communicator, he understood the need to select and express clearly and simply a very limited number of priorities in order to maximize public understanding and support. Jimmy Carter had placed his prestige behind such an unremitting number of major policy initiatives that even his strongest supporters begged for guidance on priorities while he overwhelmed Congress with the amount of draft legislation and number of policy areas in which he wanted to move. In contrast, circumstances conspired to give Ronald Reagan a clear mandate on inflation. He chose to focus his energies so fully on that issue that his priorities were as clear to their constituents as to the legislators themselves. That clear an identification of a personally popular individual with a specific policy choice substantially raised the stakes for any legislator who might wish to oppose him.

Above all, Ronald Reagan brought to the Presidency a unique level of skill at using the medium of television. He fully understood how to project the desired personal qualities through that medium. Thus he was able to develop and reinforce his personal public support through the skill with which he projected personal confidence, sincerity, strength, balance, warmth and personal modesty. In light of the difficulties his predecessors since LBJ had projecting their own personal strengths, we can recognize how difficult a medium television is to master.

Reagan was so fully professional in his mastery of the medium that he had the skill to project a slight degree of amateurism. There was a boyish smile, a catch to the throat, an occasional hesitation of speech, and a lot of "just us folks" images. The performance was finely calibrated so that just enough vulnerability was projected to stir audience identification with his humanity, without going so far as to raise questions about his capacity for leadership. That light touch of vulnerable humanity was the means through which his audience could identify with and care about him. He well understood that one can respect the invulnerable but never love them.

Individuals who are still struggling to master the medium strive so hard to appear in control that at best they project a cold, contained quality that can easily slip into an appearance of insincerity or worse, e.g., public perceptions of the characters of Presidents Johnson, Nixon and Carter. Ford's limited ability to master the medium left an image of incompetence and bumbling that badly damaged his administration.

President Reagan's communication techniques were based on a thorough understanding of the essential characteristics of the medium and its limitations. Television's impact is emotional, not cerebral. It conveys images rather than ideas. To reach and persuade the audience, any President must engage in a marketing effort intended to find images that can resonate with the desires, hopes and values of his audience. That requires simplification of issues to thirty to sixty second spots for the news, and simplification of the way those issues are presented so that they are clear and grab audience attention. As Carter and Mondale learned to their sorrow, whenever a President or presidential candidate starts discussing a topic with a phrase about its complexity, half the audience wanders off to raid the refrigerator. (The other half follows suit if a parade of statistics ensues.)

Understanding that television is a medium of images, President Reagan did not find it necessary to master detail. His frequent misstatements were not damaging, because the image he projected was confident, strong and in charge. He clearly had his eye on the "big picture." Details could be filled in by staff. He was the executive of a complex organization, and as such clearly projected that he was responsible for setting and articulating priorities and goals rather than detail. That approach served him well in sustaining public support for his leadership, in contrast to Jimmy Carter, who projected such an involvement in detail that the public perceived him as lacking executive stature.

President Reagan understood how to use his own tools to project the image he desired, and how to create "media events" to give the impression of action. He also understood how to arrange the "visuals" for maximum effect. No fireside chats in sweaters for him—he understood that the American people expect their leader to own a suit. An example of his skill with the "visuals" was given by his 1986 State of the Union Message. The President was speaking at a podium below the Speaker of the House. As long as the camera angles were tight, the President would be in control, but when the lens zoomed back viewers would see his partisan opponent, Speaker Tip O'Neill, looking down on him with the heaviest jowls and bushiest eyebrows in American politics, registering modified rapture at the remarks.

Ronald Reagan handled that by starting with an unexpected encomium to the Speaker on his years of service, pending retirement and birthday. After leading an ovation for Tip, the President could get on with his message, secure in the knowledge that he had projected exceptional grace to an opponent and that Tip was in such a state of blushing surprise and "awe shucks" pleasure that the eyebrows and jowls were neutralized for the duration of the speech.

Similarly, the President knew the growing criticism in the country of his substantial budget cuts in programs in education, health, and those helping inner-city poor. The speech contemplated no change on these policies, but in Nancy Reagan's box three children sat: a little Black boy whose talents as a gospel singer had raised him from inner-city poverty; a little girl whose heroism had saved a classmate from the wheels of a school bus; and a teenage boy whose medical experiment had blown up in the Challenger. As the President praised them he was linked visually with their issues in an image that remained long after the words of the State of the Union Message were forgotten by most viewers.

When we consider President Reagan's success in narrowing the gap between initiative and implementation, we should consider how far the qualities of good fortune and skill will be transferrable to his successors. What are the prospects for the future?

Prospects for the Future

With the inflation issue defused, there is no single, cross-cutting political issue that can unite the nation's factions to provide a mandate for Ronald Reagan's successors. As the country returns to a more normal era of diverse issues, the Presidency will be deprived of that focus and legitimacy for action that were a hallmark of Reagan's first term. It was, indeed, beginning to crumble in his second term, where he began to tailor his requests to the "limits of the possible."

Surely his successors cannot count on the comparative international peace that President Reagan enjoyed. Oil prices are not expected to remain at the depressed levels of his early years. Naturally, we can hope that there will be no further assassination attempts, whose skillful handling contributed to Reagan's support.

In short, none of the aspects of Reagan's good fortune (with the possible exception of continued disarray in the Democratic Party) can be counted upon by his successors. Nor have any of the myriad potential candidates of either party demonstrated President Reagan's singular skill with the medium of television. All the advisors and experts in the world can never compensate for the individual's personal capacity in that regard. Many recent Presidents have had excellent media advisors, but no jockey ever carried a horse across the finish line.

Lacking Reagan's good fortune and skill, his successors of either party are likely to face the same difficulties that confronted his predecessors—the growing gap between initiative and implementation. Despite high levels of political sensitivity and effective Congressional liaison, they will continue to face great obstacles in attempting to achieve the implementation of their initiatives.

Those who desire change will find the potential for stalemate increasingly frustrating, particularly those who share in the Jeffersonian philosophy of "power to the people." On the other hand, the Federalists would be highly gratified that their system of "auxiliary precautions" continues to work so well.

Endnotes

1. Sixteen men who signed the Declaration also signed the Articles: Josiah Bartlett (N.H.); Samuel Adams, Elbridge Gerry and John Hancock (Mass.); William Ellery (R.I.); Roger Sherman, Samuel Huntington and Oliver Wolcott (Conn.); Francis Lewis (N.Y.); Jno Witherspoon (N.J.); Robert Morris (Penn.); Thomas McKean (Del.); Richard Henry Lee and Francis Lightfoot Lee (Va.); John Penn (N.C.) and Thomas Hayward, Jr. (S.C.).

2. Roger Sherman (Conn.) and Robert Morris (Penn.) signed all three documents; Benjamin Franklin, George Clymer and James Wilson (Penn.) signed the Declaration and Constitution, as did George Reed (Del.); Gouv. Morris (respectively for N.Y. and Penn.) and Daniel Carroll (Md.) signed the Articles and Constitution.

3. Hamilton in *Federalist 77*.

4. *Federalist 51*.

5. Shakespeare, *King Henry IV, Part I*, Act III, Scene I.

6. Under the rule of seniority, a committee chairman was the member of the majority party with the longest continuous service on that specific committee.

7. For a detailed list of the changes during the 1970's see Norman J. Ornstein, "The Constitution and the Sharing of Foreign Policy Responsibility," in Edmund Muskie *et. al.*, eds., *Congress, The President and Foreign Policy* (Lanham, MD: University Press of America, 1986), pp. 55–6.

8. V.O. Key, *Public Opinion and American Democracy* (New York: Alfred A. Knopf, 1961).

Supreme Court
Enforcement of Separation of Powers:
A Balance Sheet

by

J. Woodford Howard, Jr.
Thomas P. Stran Professor of Political Science
The Johns Hopkins University.

The Supreme Court of the United States has come a long way from humble origins. When it opened in 1790, few would have challenged Alexander Hamilton's prediction that the judicial department would be the "least dangerous branch" of the new national government.[1] The Justices met a day late in a borrowed chamber in the Royal Exchange Building of New York City and soon adjourned for lack of business. The first Chief Justice, John Jay, also minister to the Court of St. James, resigned in five years to run for Governor of New York and to engage in lucrative business. This suggests where the action was. Certainly on the eve of Thomas Jefferson's "second revolution" in 1801, when the organization of federal judicial power became the subject of harsh partisan conflict, few supposed that John Adams' second choice for Chief Justice, John Marshall of Virginia, would lay foundations for the tribunal's growth into the most powerful judicial body in human history.

Today, nine Justices from their "marble palace" on Capitol Hill, assisted by lower federal courts and state judges, enforce the supremacy and uniformity of national law over fifty-one legal systems, including coordinate branches of the federal government and vast bureaucracies—national, state, and local. Judges, interpreting statutes and administrative procedures, are deeply involved in making public policy across a broad range of subjects from abortion to zoning. In its most important role as a constitutional court, the Supreme Court is the authoritative interpreter of the U.S. Constitution, applying three principles of constitutional limitation—separation of powers, federalism, and individual rights—in cases brought to the tribunal. From almost 5,000 cases docketed annually in the late 1980's, the Justices decided about 150–200 cases with full argument and opinions. Roughly half concern the Constitution.

Construing the Constitution has converted the high tribunal into a "continuous constitutional convention." The Justices, armed with power to review and nullify actions of public officials as unconstitutional, legitimate as well as limit authority and define as well as enforce rights in an enormously diverse and dynamic society. Interpretation, to be sure, overlaps with other methods of constitutional growth. Amendments, notably the Bill of Rights as well as the Civil War, income tax, and women's suffrage amendments, have profoundly altered the American polity. Customs and practice, as in Britain, also flesh out the Constitution into a working government. Political parties, the scope of judicial power, and executive-congressional relations are important examples.

More than any other people, nonetheless, Americans rely on adjudication as the preferred method of constitutional development. Judicial review is one reason why the world's first written constitution remains the oldest. Incremental judicial interpretation has helped us adapt a compact designed for a developing, agrarian, and elitist republic to the needs of a post-industrial, continental, and democratic superpower with minimal alteration of the Framers' spare, original text. The Supreme Court thus mediates between forces of continuity and change; and a flexible, organic Constitution lives as an instrument of permanent, and mostly peaceful, revolution in a world where the only constant is change.

A written Constitution as paramount law and a separate judicial branch to enforce it are original American contributions to the art of free government. Indeed, they are among this country's greatest contributions to world culture. Constitutional courts have taken root in many countries and continents, particularly since World War II. That is why our bicentennial is being celebrated across the globe. Constitutional ideas of the New World, like the art of the Old, are common property of humanity.

At home, the Supreme Court has seldom escaped controversy. Whether the Court served as a brake or a motor of the body politic, critics have complained about the political and personal nature of its authority, that judicial review itself violates federalism and separation of powers. "Impeach Earl Warren" billboards dotted the landscape after *Brown* v. *Board of Education*.[2] While Justice William J. Brennan, Jr., was receiving an honorary degree in Los Angeles recently, a plane flew over the law school with a large advertisement: "Pray for the death of baby killer Brennan."[3] Current debates between Attorney General Edwin W. Meese III and Justice Brennan over judicial activism are fairly tame by historical standards. Thomas Jefferson denounced the judiciary as "the most dangerous branch"— a "worm," "sapping by little and little the foundations of the Constitution."[4] Presidents Jefferson and Lincoln declined to enforce judicial orders. Franklin D. Roosevelt advanced a court-packing plan to "save the Constitution from the Court and the Court from itself."[5] To Charles Evans Hughes' concession that "we live under a Constitution, but the Constitution is what the judges say it is," Senator Hugo L. Black added: "at the time they last say it."[6] The plot of a 1937 musical perhaps had the last word when the Supreme Court struck down the Constitution as unconstitutional.

The task of this study is to assess the role of the Supreme Court in enforcing the constitutional allocation of powers within the national government. This assessment is made in light of a larger question: What is the future of constitutionalism—the concept of free government under law—during an era of giant government and chronic international crisis? Americans today, as in the past, are ambivalent about separation of powers. Respected figures voice perennial criticism that diffusion of authority cripples us in making effective domestic and foreign policy.[7] On the contrary, defenders rejoin, the lesson of the Watergate and Iran-Contra scandals is that following "the Constitution could protect us from our worst mistakes."[8] What can judges do to curb abuses of necessarily expanding powers, without abusing their own, in a dangerous world?

For clarity, this study begins with a statement of basic premises, a disclaimer, and the thesis. Previous essays establish essential starting points. The Framers of the Constitution, while strengthening national government, relied mainly on politics and institutional structures to preserve liberty. The main structural limits on national authority were the principles of enumerated and separated powers. Federal officials could exercise only powers the sovereign people delegated in a written constitution. To prevent excessive concentration of authority, these enumerated powers were divided functionally among three branches that make, interpret, and execute the laws; then further diffused into complex checks and balances. The constitutional chefs at Philadelphia thus did not bake a three-layer cake but marble cake: a government of separate institutions sharing powers. To most Framers these structural devices rendered a Bill of Rights superfluous. Individual rights were commonly thought to be the province of state governments until after the Civil War.[9]

The disclaimer is that gauging the judiciary's work in separation of powers is harder than in federalism or individual rights. The Constitution's power-sharing provisions bristle with ambiguity. As Justice Robert H. Jackson observed, "Just what our forefathers did envision, or would have envisioned had they foreseen modern conditions, must be divined from materials about as enigmatic as the dreams Joseph was called upon to interpret for Pharoah."[10] A surprising poverty of clear precedents exists to guide jurists. Political accommodations have predominated over judicial resolutions of disputes about diffused powers. Then, too, the effects of judicial action or inaction are hard to measure. Because courts tend to deal with large questions in narrow ways, great issues of constitutional power remain unsettled. At the same time judges figure prominently in shifting coalitions of policy makers that cut across formal structures of government by routine methods of statutory and administrative review. Construing constitutions is only part of the job.

Within these limits of understanding, the question is whether allocation of national powers, as interpreted by courts, will cripple or save us in troubling times. If the past is prologue, the answer is neither very much, but some—and enough to take the bother. The Supreme Court is not the "balance wheel" of separation of powers, as civics texts suggest, nor was it intended to be. Political competition and accommodation are. The Supreme Court is the authoritative expositor of the Constitution, but the branch of the national government restrained most by its interpretation of separation of powers is the judiciary itself. In practice, the Court has legitimated more than limited enormous growth in the powers of Congress and President to govern. Courts can play useful, marginal roles in jurisdictional disputes between the political branches, enforcing constitutional processes within which the political titans battle, and shielding individual rights from excessive claims of authority until sober second thoughts prevail. The central nexus, nevertheless, is Presidency versus Congress. The primary controls are politics not law, the principal actors politicians not judges. Thus, beware of either-or arguments about what courts can do to curb abuse. The clearest view of the judicial role in this field, as in others, is supplementing political controls when they stalemate or weaken.

These conclusions are drawn from three areas of decision concerning constitutional allocations of power.

The Judicial Power

The Constitution grants the Supreme Court "judicial power" without defining it. The legitimacy and scope of national judicial review depend largely on interpretation. Judicial review of *state action* was expressly granted in the supremacy clause of Article VI and clearly intended in the creation of separate federal courts. The primary mission of the Supreme Court and lower federal courts is enforcing the supremacy and uniformity of national laws in the states. Practice confirms the design. The bulk of Supreme Court business— and objections to its decisions—have always concerned federalism and individual rights, not separation of powers.

Judicial review of *national action*, by contrast, is a custom of more problematic provenance. It evolved by implication from Article III. Whether the Framers intended judicial interpretations of the Constitution to bind coordinate branches of the national government will long be debated. The Court's first elaboration of the principle was Chief Justice Marshall's celebrated opinion in *Marbury* v. *Madison* (1803),[11] which implied it as corollaries of a supreme, written constitution and the judicial function. No one seriously disputed his first proposition that "an Act of the Legislature repugnant to the Constitution is void." The real question was, who decides? Marshall's answer was an oft-repeated assertion of inherent judicial power: "It is emphatically the province and duty of the judicial department to say what the law is."[12]

The problem is that Marshall's one-liner did not resolve the scope of judicial review. *Marbury* is open to two interpretations. The minimalist view, in the context of the case and cited precedents, is that the Court can protect its own turf from encroachments or enlargements by Congress and President. Virtually everyone, even Jefferson, accepts judicial review for this purpose. Seeing little magic in parchment, Jefferson thought that each co-equal branch should interpret the Constitution. Disputes that politicians could not accommodate, the people should settle by amendments or new conventions to avoid knitarchy and "rule from the grave." The maximalist view is that "the federal judiciary is supreme in the exposition of the law of the Constitution" to avoid the chaos of politicians determining their own powers and frequent resort to the people.[13] Yet, Marshall never literally claimed this power in all cases, nor nullified another national statute. His great defense of judicial review and the organic Constitution in *McCulloch* v. *Maryland* (1819),[14] addressed national supremacy over the states, not judicial supremacy over Congress and President.

History has opted for maximalism. By the twentieth century, expectations have become deeply rooted that the Supreme Court is "the ultimate interpreter of the Constitution" concerning both national and state action, subject to amendment.[15] Only five of twenty-six amendments have overturned Supreme Court decisions. None directly concerned separation of powers.

Letting courts have "the last word on the meaning of the Constitution" speaks volumes about American attitudes toward law and politics.[16] Judicial review from the start provoked perennial issues of legitimacy, capacity, and accountability in a democratic republic. Why should judges police the boundaries of power among equal branches, even at the behest of individuals, when politicians actually have settled most interbranch squabbles without chaos, as Jefferson foresaw? How can judicial review be reconciled with political democracy? It is easy to get agitated over these issues. Judge Learned Hand thought that national judicial review violated separation of powers. Justice Felix Frankfurter believed it "inherently at war with democracy."[17] A careful look at the record, however, reminds one of

Tallulah Bankhead's reaction to a play: "There's less here than meets the eye."

For one thing, the Court has struck down relatively few acts of President and Congress. Up to 1986, the Court nullified national statutes, in whole or in part, in 136 cases. This averages less than one per year. Seven times more state and local enactments (N=968) fell in the same period.[18] Very few of the national cases, moreover, involved division of powers. Of those that did, only a handful compare in social consequence to high Court actions in free speech, racial segregation, reapportionment, and abortion, which turned on different constitutional limitations.

Several reasons account for the paucity of judicial decisions regarding separation of powers. A major cluster are legal limits embedded in the Constitution itself. Article III states: "The judicial power shall extend to all Cases, in Law and Equity, arising under this Constitution, the Laws of the United States, and Treaties made... under their Authority."[19] This phrase is pregnant with limits. Deciding cases distinguishes courts from legislatures and executives. What constitutes a case is the lock and the key of federal judicial power.

The Supreme Court, importing the traditional adversary system of private adjudication into the concept of a case, has developed a string of threshold requirements controlling who may litigate what and when.[20] Consequently, the Justices have no roving commission to correct unconstitutional conduct. Courts lack a self-starter. Decision must await a properly-brought case. Because a case requires a concrete injury that courts can remedy, one of the high Court's earliest decisions was a refusal to render an "advisory opinion" requested by President George Washington about the validity of a proposed treaty.[21] For similar reasons, the Justices decline to decide claims that are too early ("unripe") or too late ("moot").

Political questions and standing are important doctrines by which life-tenured judges avoid conflict with elected branches of government. Both blend separation of powers with prudential considerations. Political questions, involving the *what* or subjects of litigation, are not questions having political significance but those which the Constitution expressly or functionally allocates to the political branches. Circularity confuses this distinction between "political" and "justiciable" questions, because judges decide which are which and their decisions are inconsistent. Despite Justice Brennan's effort to rationalize the precedents in *Baker* v. *Carr* (1962),[22] leading scholars dismiss political questions as basically policy decisions by judges to stay out of the fray. Even so, the doctrine severely limits federal judicial power, especially in foreign and national security affairs. The status of amendments, recognition of foreign states and governments, termination of wars, all these and more are "nonjustifiable."[23] A recent reminder of the potency of this doctrine occurred after Justice

Potter Stewart's death. A CBS commentator revealed that Stewart wanted the world to know that he thought American warmaking in Viet Nam was invalid without a congressional declaration of war, but that he failed to persuade enough colleagues to hear a case, much less declare an undeclared war unconstitutional.[24]

Standing governs *who* may litigate. To engage federal judicial power, a plaintiff must demonstrate a personal stake in a case, ostensibly to insure the concrete representation of private claims that the adversary process purportedly promotes. A vivid example arose from President Gerald Ford's pardon of Richard M. Nixon. The only person in the country with standing to contest the pardon in court was the special prosecutor, Leon M. Jaworski, who declined because he thought no sitting President could be constitutionally prosecuted for a crime in the first place.[25] The remedy lay in the next election.

Together, political questions and standing are formidable vehicles to avoid political thickets. In companion cases challenging an early grant-in-aid program to protect maternal health, for instance, the Court ruled that states had to challenge the constitutionality of federal expenditures in political forums. Individual taxpayers with only a general interest in the spending lacked standing to sue.[26] The combination effectively removed the Court from many controversies over budget-making, taxation, and spending.

It is no accident that threshold requirements have aroused controversy in recent decades. The Warren Court relaxed taxpayers' standing to hear religion cases and expanded representation of activist groups. The Burger Court in turn tightened some controls, provoking complaints that it slammed the courthouse door against vindication of substantive rights. Prominent prospects for the high Court in the Reagan years, Antonin Scalia and Robert H. Bork, are articulate champions of strict threshold requirements.[27] Underlying the controversy are tensions between traditional, private-right concepts of adjudication and new, public-interest concepts in which individuals and groups champion rights affecting many others. Arcane though these procedural levers may seem to nonlawyers, they enable Justices to control the volume, shape, and policy outcomes of federal litigation, not to mention the people's access to courts and the roles of judges in the constitutional scheme. To understand why the Supreme Court figures so little in perennial battles over the budget and foreign policy, these socalled technicalities are a good place to begin. In Article III, a succinct lawyers' clause of the Constitution, lurk powerful restraints on judicial power.

Informal checks also condition what courts say and do. Physical workload is a pressing constraint. The high Court's span of control stretches so thinly over so many subjects and tribunals that some experts worry about Balkanization of national law. Justices work, moreover, in a complex environment filled with political and professional restraints, both subtle and crude. Litigants initiate cases, lawyers and lower courts shape them. Five Justices are harder to convince than one. Presidents nominate, Senators confirm, and Congress controls the Court's appellate jurisdiction. That politicians rarely invoke formal checks against the Court recalls President Theodore Roosevelt's remark: "I may not know much about law, but I do know one can put the fear of God into judges."[28]

In fact, the Supreme Court is seldom at odds with dominant policy-making coalitions by virtue of political and professional screens in selection of its members. Justices are hardly indifferent to public opinion. They feel the force of their profession "like the atmosphere."[29] The delicacy and finality of their rulings have led them to develop rules of self-restraint. They normally resolve doubt in favor of government and avoid constitutional questions whenever a case can be fairly decided on other grounds. Nor should the Court formulate a rule of constitutional law broader than is required by the precise facts to which it is applied.[30] These self-denying ordinances, even if sometimes ignored, buttress the formal, physical, political, and professional constraints that inhibit judicial hegemony.

So let us draw the first subtotal of the balance sheet. (1) The Supreme Court, after a fragile start, has evolved into the authoritative interpreter of the U.S. Constitution, short of amendment. Judicial review of national and state action converts the tribunal into a continuous constitutional convention, which mediates between forces of continuity and change in a "living" Constitution. (2) The primary mission of the Supreme Court throughout American history has been to enforce the supremacy and uniformity of national law and of federally-created rights of individuals in the states. Enforcing separation of powers is secondary. (3) Notwithstanding its role as ultimate interpreter, the branch of the national government limited most by Supreme Court interpretation of separation of powers is the judiciary itself. The legitimacy of judicial review is most problematic where it has been exercised least.

Shortly before World War I, Justice Oliver Wendell Holmes commented:

> I do not think the United States would come to an end if we [the Court] lost our power to declare an Act of Congress void. I do think the Union would be imperiled if we could not make that declaration as to the laws of the several States[31]

Edward S. Corwin, a great constitutional scholar, concluded in 1952: "By and large, this still sizes up the situation."[32] So it does today.

The Executive Power

The record of judicial review of executive and legislative action suggests why Holmes, as usual, was on the beam. The bottom line is that the Supreme Court has encouraged far more than curbed the concentration of authority in the executive, which marks almost all modern governments. We no longer presume, like James Madison, that "in republican government, the legislative authority necessarily predominates."[33] The flywheel of American politics has shifted from Congress to the Presidency.

Eroded in the process are basic constitutional distinctions the Framers took for granted in distributing national powers, such as domestic and foreign affairs, war and peace, civil and military jurisdiction. Even more fundamental has been dilution, with judicial approval, of the Framers' understanding that the national government can exercise only enumerated powers. Just as judicial review of national action has matured into constitutional custom, so Americans expect vigorous presidential leadership, the meets and bounds of which are still unfolding.

The principle that presidential authority must derive from powers enumerated or implied in Article II of the Constitution no longer contains the Presidency. One of the last Presidents to embrace this concept, William Howard Taft, regarded the chief executive as a *trustee* exercising the people's delegated powers. Since then, Presidents and their spokesmen have advanced progressively broader justifications to fit law to felt necessities at home and abroad. Theodore Roosevelt contended that the President, as a *steward* of the people, should do whatever national needs demand except acts the Constitution and laws expressly forbid. During World War II, Franklin D. Roosevelt came close to the *prerogative* theory of British monarchs. Prerogative, in John Locke's words, means "power to act according to discretion for the public good, without the prescription of the law and sometimes against it."[34] Both Jefferson in the Louisiana Purchase and Lincoln in the Civil War invoked it to enlarge and defend the Union. So did Fawn Hall and her superiors in the Irancontra scandal—minus Jefferson's remedy of openly throwing oneself "on the justice of his country and the rectitude of his motives."[35]

Pioneering expansions of executive authority are increasingly justified by theories of *inherent* power. This theory, analogous to the idea that judicial review is inherent in the judicial function, holds that the President has broad, indefinite authority inherent in the functions of chief executive, chief negotiator, and commander in chief. President Richard M. Nixon's *imperial* theory went to the logical extreme: "When the President does it, that means that it is not illegal."[36] Law is executive will.

Beyond repudiating Nixon's imperialism, the Supreme Court has neither settled the basis of, nor fundamentally arrested, the growth of executive power. Consider the record according to constitutional sources of executive authority. As Chief Justice, Taft himself invoked executive prerogative in sustaining virtually unlimited power to pardon criminal offenders.[37] Similarly, Presidents (though not subordinates) are immune from judicial orders while performing ministerial duties and from civil damage suits for their official acts.[38]

Shared treaty power is instructive. The United States, uniquely among nations, elevated treaties alongside the Constitution and federal statutes as supreme law of the land, because of embarrassing state resistance to enforcing peace treaties under the Articles of Confederation. Early in this century the Supreme Court erected the 10th Amendment and a doctrine of nondelegation of enumerated powers as barriers against domestic economic regulation. The same Justices lowered both barriers to validate foreign agreements. In an early environmental protection case, *Missouri v. Holland* (1920)[39], the Court held that the national government had power to regulate migratory birds in the states as an incident of treaty making, which it lacked as an incident of power to regulate interstate commerce. The Court then approved executive agreements that preempted state laws governing private property confiscated during the Russian Revolution as an incident of President Roosevelt's authority to recognize foreign governments. These cases applied classic principles that in foreign affairs "state lines disappear."[40]

The hitch is that executive agreements also by-pass the Senate, traditional guardian of state interests. While the Court has never squarely decided whether executive agreements poach on Senate prerogatives, thousands of such agreements poach on Senate prerogatives, thousands of such agreements exist.

Fears of unfettered presidential discretion roiled into a full-scale assault on these decisions after World War II. The controversy cooled after the proposed Bricker Amendment to overturn them failed by one vote in the Senate and the Supreme Court declared that the Bill of Rights protected service-related civilians stationed abroad.[41] Even so, weakening domestic restraints in the conduct of foreign policy and emphasizing individual rights over federalism and separation of powers illuminate the high Court's postwar priorities.

The Supreme Court itself gave a powerful boost to the doctrine of inherent powers of presidents in foreign affairs. The seminal case is *United States v. Curtiss-Wright Export Corp.* (1936),[42] which sustained Congress's delegation to President Roosevelt of power to punish by criminal sanctions arms sales during a war between Paraguay and Bolivia. To circumvent the ban on excessive delegation, the Court embraced Justice George Sutherland's theory that *external* sovereignty passed directly from Great Britain to the Union of states as a concomitant of nationality, whereas *internal* sovereignty lodged in the states. In addition, Sutherland stressed "the very delicate, plenary and exclusive power of the President as the sole organ of the federal government in the field of international relations."[43] While Sutherland conceded that constitutional limits controlled Presidents, this theory undercut the Framers' fundamental principles of popular sovereignty and enumerated powers in a written constitution, principles on which judicial review itself depends.

Sutherland's loose language, vaulting the President's role of sole negotiator into foreign-policy chief, is a touchstone for advocates of executive supremacy in foreign affairs. Like Theodore Roosevelt's stewardship theory, it shifts the question from what the Constitution grants to what it expressly forbids. Anything less goes. Despite Sutherland's confusion of international and constitutional law, the Supreme Court still embraces his concept of executive authority and thereby contributes, in my view, to a dangerous misconception rising in American constitutionalism: personification of the nation's sovereignty in the Presidency.[44]

The Framers, rebels and realists about human frailty, clearly envisaged power-sharing in starting and waging war. While they sought a vigorous executive and made the President commander in chief to insure civilian supremacy, they realized with George Mason that nothing was more dangerous than uniting purse and sword in the same hands. To guard against standing armies and foreign adventurism, historic banes of monarchy, the delegates at Philadelphia initially granted Congress power both to raise armies and to "make" war. They amended "make" to "declare" war for fear of hobbling executive responses to foreign attack.

This exception has now swallowed the rule. It scarcely exaggerates to say that modern Presidents have power to get us into wars and to become virtual "constitutional dictators" to win them, at least in total conflicts like World War II.[45] How to balance liberty and security in the blurred, middle ground of quasi-war, quasi-peace is the greatest challenge to constitutionalism today.

The Constitution's provisions about starting wars once had force. During the Civil War, while upholding President Lincoln's blockade of Southern ports, the Supreme Court advanced an "open court" rule to test the legality of warlike acts before a congressional declaration of war. So long as courts were open to defend legal rights, the Court reasoned, Congress must declare war.[46]

The open-court principle was abandoned in our century as hopelessly romantic. Presidents dispatched armed forces to Korea, Vietnam, Iran, Lebanon, Grenada, Libya and the Persian Gulf without congressional approval. Legislative power to declare war has fallen victim to changing technology and concepts of warfare. Presidents must react to atomic attack before Congress could obey a quorum call.

Indeed, legislators struggle just to be informed, let alone consulted about executive initiatives that threaten hostilities. After the Vietnam war, Congress enacted carefully-crafted statutes to reclaim a role in these policies without crippling Presidents. The War Powers

Resolution of 1973 defined situations in which forces may be committed abroad and imposed timely reporting requirements. Congress also required reporting of foreign arms sales and covert intelligence activities. Presidents claim that the War Powers Act is unconstitutional and ineffective against terrorism. President Reagan's staff allegedly ignored and lied to Congress about arms sales and covert operations during the Iran-contra affair. The Supreme Court has not passed on these statutes, but they illustrate grave constitutional problems. Are legal controls on executive secrecy and discretion compatible with a world power's responsibilities? Can we advance democracy abroad by sacrificing it at home?

Presidents rarely lack authority to wage war. Congress usually delegates vast powers to the executive during emergencies over and above the President's own pools of power. The latter are elastic, though not limitless. The Constitution presumes congressional authority to declare martial law but restricts suspension of the writ of habeas corpus to cases of rebellion or invasion. The powers of the commander in chief originally were understood as command of military forces, implying no authority over civilians.[47] After the Civil War, a unanimous Court ruled in *ex parte Milligan* (1867)[48] that Lincoln alone could not suspend the writ of habeas corpus; and a 5–4 majority argued that neither could President and Congress together so long as federal courts were open and functioning.

These controls bit the dust during World War II. In the Japanese Relocation Program on the West Coast the government retained, relocated, and incarcerated 120,000 persons of Japanese ancestry—70,000 of them U.S. citizens—on grounds of military necessity. The Supreme Court ignored the lack of martial law and open courts and approved the curfew and relocation under the principle of judicial deference to expert findings that it was impossible to segregate immediately "the disloyal from the loyal."[49]

In upholding wholesale violations of civil liberties, these oft-criticized decisions vastly extended the commander in chief's authority to civilians without martial law. It is now generally conceded that the military judgments to which the Justices deferred were tainted with racism, as Justice Murphy eloquently charged in dissent. The decisions are currently under legal attack for alleged government misconduct in withholding vital information from the Court refuting military necessity.[50] However these appeals turn out, one should ponder the high Court's sweeping definition of authority. War power is the "power to wage war successfully," wrote Chief Justice Stone; and when exercised by those on whom the Constitution places the responsibility of warmaking, no court should "sit in review of the wisdom of their action or substitute its judgment for theirs."[51] Phoenix-like, Stone's denunciation of racism planted the seed of strict scrutiny in equal protection that contradicts "no review." The Court's deference to group guilt in wartime, as Justice Jackson warned, nevertheless stands like a "loaded weapon ready for the hand of any authority that can bring forward a plausible claim of urgent need."[52]

The whole World War II experience, to be sure, cannot be captured by its worst case. Generally speaking, the government did a better job protecting free speech, press, and religion than in World War I. Justice Wiley Rutledge's perceptive dissent against invasion of judicial power in a price-control case, *Yakus* v. *United States*, (1944),[53] persuaded Congress to make amends. Still, in only one case interpreting the treason clause did the Supreme Court restrict war powers on constitutional grounds during this conflict.[54] And that decision, like *Milligan*, came near the end when idealism brimmed.

World War II was chillingly counter-productive for judicial limits on executive power. The lessons of total war were that the President as "sole organ" of foreign policy and as commander in chief has virtually a free hand to start and wage wars. Congress delegated vast war powers to the President, who shifted them to civilian and military officials. The Supreme Court, finding itself "powerless in fact," declared itself "powerless in law."[55] The United States, coming of age as the world's mightiest power, was hardly exempt from an old adage: "When war comes, the law goes."

Judicial power revived during lesser emergencies of the Korean War and Watergate. Two great cases—*Youngstown Sheet and Tube Co.* v. *Sawyer* (1952)[56] and *United States* v. *Nixon* (1974)[57]— became significant symbolic victories for the rule of law. Both rejected bald assertions by counsel that a President's aggregate or inherent powers are beyond judicial review. A careful look at each decision, however, again discloses less than meets the eye.

In *Youngstown*, the Court invalidated executive "seizure"of steel mills to prevent a strike and an ammunition shortage during the Korean War. A paradox of voting appears in the Court's complex line-up. Though five Justices supported Justice Black's simplistic opinion for the Court that seizure invaded legislative functions, the controlling fact for four members of the six-man majority was that Congress had considered and rejected the remedy of seizure for emergency labor disputes, thus preempting the field. Since three dissenters thought the seizure lawful anyhow, all but Black and Douglas left open the great issue of aggregate executive powers to act alone in emergencies when Congress is silent.

This overblown constitutional crisis reduced to a statutory preemption case. And the parties settled the dispute on terms informally agreed to before seizure.[58] Corwin and others dismissed the decision, accordingly, as "a judicial brick without straw."[59] In retrospect, *Youngstown* is more than that. Legally, it supports the proposition that chief executives lack inherent power to set domestic, legislative policy contrary to the will of Congress. In the Cold War context, it was an important symbolic step in reviving judicial checks against expansion of executive powers domestically as an offshoot of power to wage limited war. President Truman himself repudiated his lawyers' contentions in district court of boundless executive authority; his Solicitor General conceded that Presidents lack seizure power that Congress denied or disapproved.[60]

The case inspired Justice Jackson to write perhaps the greatest modern analysis of the Court's role in enforcing the flexible principle of separated powers. *Youngstown*, like *Marbury*, was a significant shot across the bow.

United States v. *Nixon* was a far more serious challenge to constitutional government. The conflict over release of taped conversations in the oval office was between the President and the courts, with Congress standing by as an indirect beneficiary. President Nixon and his lawyers, unlike Harry S. Truman, hinted that the President might not obey an adverse decision by a coequal branch. Rejecting the President's claim of absolute discretion to determine the scope of executive privilege, a unanimous Supreme Court held that the general privilege of the chief executive to confidential communications must yield to the judiciary's specific need for evidence in criminal trials.[61]

In context, this was a mighty blow for constitutionalism. Nixon's own appointees repudiated his absolutist claims. His obedience to the Court's ruling bolstered its supremacy in constitutional interpretation and returned the Presidency to the rule of law. Politically, the Court's decision tipped the balance of power, and the surrendered tapes revealed the "smoking gun" that brought him down.

This precedent is doubled-edged, all the same. Conflicts over executive privilege usually have been settled by political accommodation, as in the hearings over William Rehnquist's nomination to be Chief Justice. Nixon's case was the first time the Court recognized a constitutional basis for executive privilege in separation of powers. What is its scope? Would the outcome have differed had the taped conversations concerned the secret bombing of Cambodia, where the President acted as commander in chief and "sole organ of the nation in international relations"? Even the House Judiciary Committee rejected the bombing as grounds of impeachment in 1974.

Except for Nixon's tapes, the Burger Court consistently deferred to presidential power in foreign and national security affairs. The Court held that the former President enjoyed "absolute immunity from civil damage claims predicated upon his official acts."[62] It refused to decide whether President Carter could constitutionally abrogate a defense treaty with Taiwan without Senate approval.[63] Emphasizing congressional acquiescence in the Iranian Assets Case, it sustained an executive agreement transferring claims in American courts to an Iran-U.S. special claims tribunal.[64] It approved executive bans on Cuban travel.[65] The Rehnquist Court barred suits by military personnel against the government for violating constitutional rights and overruled Warren Court rulings that they cannot be court-martialed for nonservice-connected offenses.[66] Rehnquist is a forceful exponent of judicial deference to presidential discretion and military jurisdiction in national security affairs. Initial signs point to Justice Scalia as a kindred spirit.

The controversy to watch from the Iran-contra scandal is control over covert intelligence activities. Did President Reagan and his staff violate the Boland Amendment prohibiting government military aid to Nicaraguan contras during periods specified by Congress? Reagan at first denied any knowledge that officials in the National Security Council sponsored and supported a private and foreign network of aid to the contras. Then, conceding the facts—"It was my idea to begin with"—the President and his spokesmen retreated to legal defenses that the statute (1) applied only to intelligence services and (2) unconstitutionally trenched on the President's control of foreign policy. Editors have squared-off with vigorous constitutional debate. Calling Reagan a lawless executive, the *New York Times* charged that the end-run around Congress violated the President's duty to faithfully execute the laws.[67] The *Wall Street Journal* declared the Boland Amendment a "patently unconstitutional" invasion of his powers as commander in chief.[68] Let us now draw the executive subtotal. (1) The Supreme Court has validated rather than restricted the growth of executive power. What were once viewed as formidable obstacles to presidential hegemony—the principle of enumerated powers, Congress' power to declare war, the Senate's check on international agreements, the process of martial law, the concept of the commander in chief as a purely military officer—have all eroded with judicial blessing during the rise of the United States as a super-power. The philosophy underlying the fading of these structural safeguards of liberty within the national government is the same that justifies the trend toward a unitary state in economic life and civil rights: "The power is as broad as the need that evokes it."[69]

(2) Still, the Supreme Court has not abdicated. The question is not whether judges are powerless to curb executive abuses but whether they can contribute something worthwhile. The *Youngstown* and *Nixon* cases suggest what that something is. The Supreme Court can play useful marginal roles, helping to keep political branches within prescribed limits and enforcing the groundrules under which political titans battle. As traffic cops of the political process, courts have repudiated unbridled presidential imperialism, cleaned up messy statutes, and staunched the spillover of foreign policy power into domestic spheres, at least in peacetime. Distinguishing between foreign and domestic wiretapping is a related example under the 4th Amendment.[70] Flexible powers can be calibrated to cushion their impact on individuals. Moreover, some of the judiciary's most effec-

tive restraints against executive abuses, such as immigration and industrial security cases, occur in nonglamorous, nonconstitutional, routine supervision of the millions who act in the name of the President.[71] The judiciary thus supplements rather than supplants the political controls on which we rely most for protection against arbitrary government.

When push comes to constitutional shove, however, neither Congress nor Court is willing to tie the hands of Presidents to meet unforseen emergencies. Clinton Rossiter's warning still rings true:

> We delude ourselves cruelly if we count on the Court at all hopefully to save us from the consequences of most abuses of presidential power. The fact is that the Court has done more over the years to expand than to contract the authority of the Presidency....[72]

The Legislative Power

The framers, assuming congressional dominance, worried more about controlling legislative than presidential encroachments. So has the modern Supreme Court, notwithstanding the shift to executive dominance. Judicial oversight of Congress under the separation of powers has centered on diverse problems which, for convenience, may be grouped into two broad categories: (1) internal governance of each house and their members, such as legislative investigations and immunities; and (2) interbranch power-sharing by delegation, vetoes, appointments and removals. Collectively, these largely procedural problems are the cutting edge of a resurgent judicial activism, conservative-style, that raises significant issues regarding who controls the bureaucracy and the scope of political accountability.

The Constitution expressly grants to each house of Congress power to determine its own rules and to punish members for misconduct. Courts traditionally have been reluctant to intervene in Congress' internal governance. Sometimes that is a hard lesson to learn. During the McCarthy era, many students yearned for the early Warren Court to curb abuses of congressional investigations. Yet the Justices reaffirmed the implied and *inherent* powers of Congress to investigate for the purposes of legislating and informing the public. Except for expanding the privilege against self-incrimination,the only constitutional limitations they imposed were that witnesses must be informed of the relevance of questions to a legitimate legislative inquiry before being compelled to answer them. Politicians, far more than judges, have worked out the groundrules of legislative investigations, then and since.

Subsequent Courts grew bolder. In *Powell* v. *McCormack* (1969),[73] the Justices held that the House could *expel* but not *exclude* a reelected member who met the Constitution's age, citizenship, and residency requirements. Chief Justice Warren's last big opinion reversed the view of his nominated successor, Warren E. Burger, that the issue was a political question.

The Burger Court, rejecting arguments that Congress is the sole judge of a legislator's immunities for statements under the speech and debate clause, engaged in extensive line-drawing over the reach of this privilege. Senator Mike Gravel and his aide, for instance, were immune from grand-jury questioning about disclosure (though not commercial publication) of the Pentagon papers.[74] And Wisconsin's budget-watching Senator, William Proxmire, became subject to a libel suit for giving a "Golden Fleece of the Month Award" to an animal researcher whose studies, the Senator wrote in a newsletter, "made a monkey of the American taxpayer."[75]

The major growing points in constitutional allocation of powers today concern delegated legislative authority and appointments of independent executive officials. In the theory of enumerated and separated powers, the functions or powers delegated by the people to one branch cannot be redelegated to another. Nor should any branch have "overruling influence" in the exercise of another's functions. Their predecessors having bent the principle of nondelegation, as we shall see, the current Justices now grapple with the principle of noninterference.

Even before World War I, the high Court recognized that extensive delegation of lawmaking power was necessary for modern regulation. Just as Congress could not cover every detail in statutes, so effective administration of the laws required flexible discretion. Against claims that Congress delegated too much power, the Court seemed satisfied if the statute imposed standards to guide executive discretion. In practice the guidelines—e.g., establish peace or further the public interest-were opaque fig leaves. The only statutes ever voided for excessive delegation were a few, hastily-drafted New Deal measures. The most notable was the National Industrial Recovery Act under which industry-wide boards containing representatives of private groups wrote wage and price controls sanctioned by criminal penalties. For private persons to define crimes, Justice Cardozo declared in the *Schechter* case, was "delegation running riot."[76]

The doctrine of excessive delegation became moribund as Congress delegated vast rule-making authority to executive agencies during the last half-century. Worry persists whether the federal bureaucracy is a "headless" fourth branch of government, "which deranges our three-branch legal theories."[77] Though strong arguments can be made that continuing adaptation of bureaucracy and the political system render derangement a myth, politicians of every hue demand greater control of bureaucracy without sacrificing its advantages of efficiency and expertise.[78]

The real question is how. Three methods engage the courts. One is the bipartisan regulatory agency, like the Federal Reserve Board or the Securities and Exchange Commission, which exercizes overlapping powers independently of direct control by either Congress or President. Another device, the legislative veto, enables Congress to supervise its delegated power by reserving to one or both houses, and sometimes their committees, a veto over proposed administrative rules before they become law. A third method, popular among both New Dealers and new conservatives of the 1980s, is full political control and accountability. In this view, legislators should make the basic social judgments and administrators should be removable by the President without cause. If elected officials lack political will to make hard policy choices, nonelected bureaucrats and judges should not fill the void. As part of their deregulation agenda, conservatives in the Department of Justice attack both independent commissions and legislative vetoes as unconstitutional invasions of executive power. What is more, they have struck responsive judicial chords.

Advocates of strict construction scored a triumph in *Immigration and Naturalization Service* v. *Chadha* (1983).[79] In a sweeping decision, a 7–2 majority struck down a single-house veto of a suspended deportation order and by implication all legislative vetoes that did not follow the "step by step, deliberate, and deliberative process" that the Constitution prescribed: passage by both houses of Congress and presentment to the President for approval or veto.[80] Such short cuts, Chief Justice Burger reasoned, intruded on the President's functions in approving and executing laws. Without empirical analysis of intrusions on executive operations in different circumstances, the Court in one swoop sounded the death knell for legislative vetoes in over 200 statutes, invalidating more enactments than in the republic's entire history.

Justice White's sophisticated dissent underscored the dilemma of bureaucratic accountability to Congress. If a veto to retain legislative oversight of delegated power undercuts the executive's role in lawmaking, the Court left Congress with a Hobson's choice of no delegation or no strings. At first glance, *Chadha* greatly enhances executive power. The modern Court's position seems to be minimal scrutiny of too much delegation, strict scrutiny of too little. Even the War Powers Act may be in jeopardy. What *Chadha* portends remains uncertain, however. We should not underestimate the capacity of government organizations and political coalitions to work around onerous formal rules. Reactions range from compliance and correcting legislation to evasion. That the principle cuts both ways became plain when a lower federal court ruled that delegated authority to *impound* appropriated funds does not include power to *defer* spending.[81] *Chadha* produced one surprise. Some Justices expected an uproar on Capitol Hill. A member of the majority recently noted, "There hasn't been a peep, except for one freshman Congressman."[82]

Judicial controls on appointments and removals of personnel are closely related to delegation. To reinforce separation of powers, the Constitution provides that the President shall nominate and, with the advice and consent of the Senate, appoint ambassadors, judges, and "all other Officers of the United States." Congress is authorized to vest appointment of "such inferior Officers, as they think proper, in the President alone, in the Courts of Law, or in the Heads of Departments."[83] Except for impeachments, nothing was said about removals. The main questions requiring interpretation concern who are officers of the U.S. as distinct from inferior officers? Are removals coextensive with appointments?

In *Buckley* v. *Valeo* (1976),[84] the Burger Court held that the Federal Election Commission was defectively composed because the exercise of extensive rulemaking, adjudicative, and executive functions can only be exercised by officers of the United States, appointed accordingly, not by inferior officers chosen in part by the President *pro tem* of the Senate and the Speaker of the House. Congress quickly repaired the defect, but the coupling of selection procedures and functions provided the tool by which the Court struck down the automatic, spending-cut mechanism of the Gramm-Rudman-Hollings Act in 1986. In *Bowsher* v. *Synar* (1986)[85] the Court held that this statute invalidly gave executive powers to order budget reductions to a legislative officer, the Comptroller General. While Justice White lamented the "distressingly formalistic" approach to this hybrid office in Chief Justice Burger's last opinion for the Court, critics welcomed the statute's demise in restoring political responsibility of the President and Congress in budget making.[86]

The combination of *Chadha*, *Buckley*, and *Bowsher* may reopen a major issue settled fifty years ago: the constitutionality of independent agencies. After initially upholding plenary executive power to remove at will anyone the President appoints, the Court in the *Humphrey's Executor* case (1934)[87] restricted presidential removal for policy reasons to purely executive officers. Hence, Congress could restrict removals to specified causes such as inefficiency in order to preserve the independence of quasilegislative, quasi-judicial functions of the Federal Trade Commission from executive control. Attorney General Meese, who blames this decision for resulting in "a new and politically unaccountable fourth branch of government," contends that *Chadha* undermined its logic and other laws insulating independent agencies from presidential direction.[88] "Power granted to Congress should be properly understood as power granted to the Executive," he said. "It should be up to the President to enforce the law."[89]

The government argued similarly in the *Bowsher* case that only officials who serve at the pleasure of the President could order him to sequester funds. The Justices avoided this delegation argument; but

Justice Scalia appeared to embrace it in the lower court, and the oral argument before the high tribunal was revealing.[90] When the Comptroller General's counsel, Lloyd N. Cutler, contended that the government's position would take the Federal Reserve Board and other independent agencies "over the side with you," Solicitor General Charles Fried, distinguishing cases, dismissed the charge as "a scare." "I'll confess you scared me," Justice O'Connor remarked.[91] And well she might.

The philosophy of the new conservatives is that only courts can be independent of direct political control. Their legal strategy is to reverse *Humphrey's Executor* and perhaps to revive *Schechter.* Whoever occupies the White House after 1988, these issues are unlikely to go away. Justices Rehnquist and Scalia have urged that the excessive delegation doctrine is "worth hewing from the ice."[92] The Court's newest member, Anthony M. Kennedy, wrote the circuit court opinion that was upheld in *Chadha.* In cases currently filed, the architects of *Chadha* challenge the Federal Trade Commission's investigation of the title insurance industry as an unconstitutional invasion of executive authority.[93] Senator John Melcher, Democrat of Montana, challenges the composition of one of the world's most powerful bodies, the Open Market Committee of the Federal Reserve Board, because 5 of its 12 members are chosen by directors of regional Federal Reserve banks that include private bankers.[94] That Senators lack standing to sue in such cases, as Judge Robert H. Bork contended, itself raises substantial problems in the separation of powers.[95]

A major showdown over shared powers may result in 1988 from the Supreme Court's expedited review of a D.C. circuit decision invalidating court-appointed prosecutors under the Ethics in Government Act. Ever since this popular device was enacted after the Watergate scandal to combat conflicts of interest in the executive branch, Republican administrations have attacked independent counsel as unconstitutional intruders on exclusive executive authority to investigate and prosecute federal crimes. Accenting separation of functions, circuit judges Laurence H. Silberman and Stephen F. Williams totally rejected judicial participation. Accenting checks and balances, circuit judge Ruth Bader Ginsburg countered in dissent that the statute's careful blend of mutual checks was "faithful to the 18th-century blueprint, yet fitting for our time."[96]

Are independent counsel "officers of the United States" or "inferior officers"? On such seemingly small questions, the judiciary's checking role may depend. In view of express language in the appointments clause, not to mention precedents of courtappointed prosecutors, it is hard to believe that the great principles of separate but overlapping powers on which the framers relied most to curb arbitrary government requires officials accused of wrongdoing to investigate and prosecute themselves. With all respect, the independent counsel cases pose questions of degree.[97]

Whatever their outcome, the controversy over independent power centers illuminates enduring tensions in our constitutional system: strict vs. loose construction, formalism vs. adaptation, and instrumental theory in service of political goals. No generation has escaped such choices. Madison had to defend checks and balances against criticism that they undercut separation of powers. Jefferson held conflicting views of executive authority in and out of office. In the last half-century many conservatives and liberals have switched sides regarding Hamiltonian conceptions of presidential power and counterweights in Congress and courts. Is the issue merely who occupies the White House? Or does it tap deeper American premises that every power requires a counterpart check? Justice Jackson once observed, "The greatest principle of law I know is 'it depends on whose ox gets gored.'"[98]

The Burger Court was unusually active in policing dispersed national powers. Novel issues confront its successor. Judicial scrutiny of legislative action under this principle of constitutional limitation can be summarized in four ways. (1) The Supreme Court has generously supported implied and inherent powers considered necessary to legislative functions and selfgovernance (congressional investigations and immunities). (2) The Court has expanded judicial review over procedural innovations and found important short cuts wanting (exclusion of members, legislative vetoes). (3) The growing points of constitutional law center on ostensibly technical issues of delegation, appointments, and removals. The basic issue is who controls the federal bureaucracy. Regardless of whether the federal bureaucracy is a fourth arm or an atomizer of national government, *Chadha, Buckley,* and *Bowsher* add up to substantial victories for proponents of executive supremacy at the expense of congressional oversight and independent agents in the execution of public policy. (4) Since the Nixon Administration, the Supreme Court has applied separation of powers to limit Congress more than the President. If the conservative program to place administrative agencies under presidential control succeeds in court, the likely effects are a further concentration of authority in the White House and greater reliance on political over judicial controls in enforcing the apportionment of national powers.

A Balance Sheet

Separation of powers plus checks and balances are the most important structural controls on the national government. In practice, they tend to be the least important constitutional limitations on the agenda of the Supreme Court—except for itself. Despite expectations of judicial supremacy in interpreting the Constitution, the judiciary remains the weakest branch within the central government.

The Supreme Court's role in enforcing the allocation of national powers pales in comparison to its performance in federalism and individual rights. In federalism, enforcing the supremacy and uniformity of national laws, the high Court is not an umpire so much as a ball player on the federal team. In individual rights, creative leadership by the Court during the last half-century launched a virtual revolution in civil rights, making more equal in law the less equal in life. On the world stage, the Supreme Court is the prototype of constitutional adjudication as an instrument of social reform.

American society would change substantially if judges vacated these fields to politicians. Is that true for separation of powers? A central question is how much we should rely on law or politics to maintain the constitutional scheme. On the premise that competition for power by politicians suffices to preserve the system of divided and overlapping authority, Jesse H. Choper proposes that the Supreme Court decline to police interbranch disputes except in self-defense, the better to protect individual rights where political checks are weak.[99] Choper's proposal highlights how marginal is our balance sheet.

The primary role of the Supreme Court in separation of powers is symbolic—legitimation, not limitation. Saying yes far outweighs saying no in the growth of national power. The Court's restraints on other branches are largely procedural, not substantive. Some might say insubstantial if we compare a ruling like *Bowsher* with claims of plenary executive power to involve the country in foreign wars and insurrections, about which Justices are silent.[100] The Court can obstruct the popular branches for awhile, as in the New Deal era. It can help stabilize constitutional conflicts between them, tipping the balance of power, as in the *Youngstown* and *Nixon* affairs. In policing dispersed powers, it can enforce groundrules under which politicians compete and occasionally reenforce political responsibility of both branches, as in *Bowsher*. Federal judges increasingly participate, along with other public and private organizations, in the seamless web of lawmaking in the administrative state, thus pluralizing bureaucratic authority in the real world of Washington. As one newly-appointed, regulatory commissioner discovered to his horror in the Carter Administration, "I'm in bed with the Court of Appeals everyday!" That is why conservatives demand executive control of administrative agencies, just as cognoscenti call for more discriminating and less absolutist opinions from the Court than in *Youngstown* or *Chadha*.[101]

The sum of these contributions is supplementing, not supplanting, the political process. To answer the original straw man question—will the Constitution as enforced by courts cripple us or save us?—the short answer is neither. The Supreme Court contributes usefully but marginally to enforcement of separation of powers. Its great trump as the Constitution's final expositor is held largely in reserve. What judicial review contributes most to a free society is enforcing the constitutional limitations which by design and process suit the judiciary best: federalism and individual rights. Since the framing of the covenant, federal-state relations and individual rights have dominated the attention of the Supreme Court, its friends and its enemies. Who would change that mission in the decades ahead?

Endnotes

1. Alexander Hamilton, *The Federalist Papers*, Number 78 (New York: Mentor, 1961), 465. I am grateful for the aid of Francis E. Rourke and Mark Rush.
2. 347 U.S. 483 (1954).
3. *National Law Journal*, 16 June 1986, p. 14.
4. "The Jefferson-Korais Correspondence," *Journal of Modern History* 14 (March, 1942).
5. Quoted in Alpheus T. Mason, *Free Government in the Making* (New York: Oxford University Press, 1949), 793.
6. *Addresses and Papers of Charles Evans Hughes*, 2d ed. (New York: G. P. Putnam's Sons, 1916), 185–186. Black, quoted in *Congressional Record*, 29, March 1937, p. 2833.
7. James S. Sundquist, *Constitutional Reform and Effective Government* (Washington, D.C.: The Brookings Institution, 1986); Donald L. Robinson, ed., *Reforming American Government* (Boulder: Westview Press, 1985).
8. *Civil Liberties* (Winter, 1987), p. 12.
9. Herbert J. Storing, "The Constitution and the Bill of Rights," in M. Judd Harmon, ed. *Essays on the Constitution of the United States* (Port Washington, N.Y.: Kennikat Press Corp., 1978), 32.
10. *Youngstown Sheet & Tube Co.* v. *Sawyer*, 343 U.S. 579, 634 (1952).
11. 5 U.S. (1 Cranch) 137 (1803).
12. *Ibid.*, 158.
13. Merrill D. Peterson, "Thomas Jefferson and the Constitution," *this Constitution* (Winter, 1986), p. 12. Jesse H. Choper, *Judicial Review and the National Political Process* (Chicago: University of Chicago Press, 1980), 266–70, 385–86 n. 10, 13. From a large literature, see, e.g., Henry P. Monaghan, "Constitutional Adjudication: the Who and When," *Yale Law Journal* 82 (June, 1973): 1363, 1365; Henry M. Hart and Herbert Wechsler, *Federal Courts and the Federal System*, 2d ed. (Mineola, N.Y.: Foundation Press, 1973), 455; William W. Van Alstyne, "A Critical Guide to *Marbury* v. *Madison*," *Duke Law Journal* (1969): 1; Susan Low Bloch and Maeva Marcus, "John Marshall's Selective Use of History in *Marbury* v. *Madison*," *Wisconsin Law Review* (1986): 301; cf. Christopher Wolfe, *The Rise of Modern Judicial Review from Constitutional Interpretation to Judge-made Law* (New York: Basic Books, 1986). 14. Quote, *Cooper* v. *Aaron*, 358 U.S. 1, 18 (1958).
14. 17 U.S. (4 Wheat.) 316 (1819).
15. *Powell* v. *McCormack*, 395 U.S. 486, 521 (1969).

16. William J. Brennan, Jr., "The Constitution of the United States: Contemporary Ratification," address at Georgetown University, 12 October 1985, p. 15.

17. Learned Hand, *The Bill of Rights* (Cambridge: Harvard University Press, 1958), 1–30. *Dennis* v. *United States*, 341 U.S. 494, 517 (1951).

18. David M. O'Brien, *Storm Center* (New York: W. W. Norton & Company, Inc., 1986), 43.

19. *U.S. Constitution*, Art. III, sec. 2.

20. Monaghan, "Constitutional Adjudication."

21. Julius Goebel, Jr., *I History of the Supreme Court of the United States* (New York: The Macmillan Company, 1971), 554–557.

22. 369 U.S. 186 (1962).

23. Louis Henkin, "Is There a Political Question Doctrine?" *Yale Law Journal* 85 (1976): 597; Fritz Scharpf, "Judicial Review and the Political Question: A Functional Analysis," *Yale Law Journal* 75 (1966): 17.

24. *Baltimore Sun*, 9 December 1985, p. 3A. See *Mora* v. *McNamara*, 389 U.S. 934 (1967); *Holtzman* v. *Schlesinger*, 414 U.S. 1304, 1316 (1973).

25. Leon M. Jaworski, *Confession and Avoidance: A Memoir* (Garden City, N.Y.: Anchor Press, 1979), 209–41.

26. *Massachusetts* v. *Mellon*; *Frothingham* v. *Mellon*, 262 U.S. 447 (1923).

27. Antonin Scalia, "The Doctrine of Standing as an Element of the Separation of Powers," in Mark W. Cannon and David M. O'Brien, eds., *Views from the Bench* (Chatham, N.J.: Chatham House Publishers, Inc., 1985), 200. See Bork, J., in *Tel-Oren* v. *Libyan Arab Republic*, 726 F. 2d 774 (D.C. Cir. 1984).

28. Quoted in Archibald MacLeish and E. F. Prichard, eds., *Law and Politics and Occasional Papers of Felix Frankfurter* (New York: Capricorn Books, 1962), 15.

29. Robert A. Dahl, "Decision-Making in a Democracy: The Supreme Court as National Policy-Maker," *Journal of Public Law* 6 (1957): 284–286. Benjamin Cardozoa, *The Growth of the Law* (New Haven: Yale University Press, 1924), 61.

30. *Ashwander* v. *TVA*, 297 U.S. 288, 346 (1936).

31. Oliver Wendell Holmes, "Law and the Court," in *Collected Legal Papers* (New York: Harcourt, Brace and Howe, Inc., 1920), 295–96.

32. Edward S. Corwin, *The Constitution of the United States of America, annotated* (Washington, D.C.: U.S. Government Printing Office, 1953), xxviii.

33. Madison, *Federalist*, No. 51, 322.

34. Edward S. Corwin, *The President: Office and Powers* (New York: New York University Press, 1957); John Locke, *Two Treatises of Civil Government* (New York: Everyman's Library, 1924), 160.

35. Fawn Hall, quoted in *New York Times*, 14 June 1986, p. E24. Thomas Jefferson, Letter to J. B. Colvin, 20 September 1810, in Mason, *Free Government in the Making*, 348.

36. Quoted in Craig R. Ducat and Harold W. Chase, *Constitutional Interpretation*, 3d ed. (New York: West Publishing Company, 1983), 286.

37. *Ex parte Grossman*, 267 U.S. 87 (1925).

38. *Mississippi* v. *Johnson*, 71 U.S. (4 Wall.) 475 (1837); *Nixon* v. *Fitzgerald*, 457 U.S. 731 (1982).

39. 252 U.S. 416. For foreign affairs generally, see Louis Henkin, *Foreign Affairs and the Constitution* (Mineola, N.Y.: Foundation Press, 1972).

40. *United States* v. *Belmont*, 301 U.S. 324, 331 (1937); *United States* v. *Pink*, 315 U.S. 203 (1942).

41. *Reid* v. *Covert*, 354 U.S. 1 (1957).

42. 299 U.S. 304 (1936).

43. *Ibid.*, 320.

44. Charles A. Lofgren, "*U.S.* v. *Curtiss-Wright Export Corp.*: An Historical Reassessment," *Yale Law Journal* 83 (1973): 1.

45. Edward S. Corwin, *Constitutional Revolution, Ltd.* (Claremont, Ca.: Claremont Colleges, 1941); see Corwin, *Total War and Constitution* (New York: A. A. Knopf, 1947).

46. *The Prize Cases*, 2 Black 635 (1863).

47. Hamilton, *Federalist*, No. 69, 418. 48. 71 U.S. (4 Wall.) 2 (1866).

49. *Hirabayashi* v. *United States*, 320 U.S. 81 (1943); *Korematsu* v. *United States*, 323 U.S. 214, 219 (1944).

50. *Hohri* v. *United States*, 107 S. Ct. 2246 (1987), *Hirabayashi* v. *United States*, 828 F. 2d 591 (95h Cir. 1987); Peter H. Irons, *Justice at War* (New York: Oxford University Press, 1983).

51. *Hirabayashi* v. *United States*, 323 U.S. 81, 93 (1943).

52. *Korematsu* v. *United States*, 323 U.S. 214, 246 (1944).

53. 321 U.S. 414, 460 (1944).

54. J. Woodford Howard., Jr., "Advocacy in Constitutional Choice: The *Cramer* Treason Case," *American Bar Foundation Research Journal* 3 (1986): 375.

55. Clinton L. Rossiter, *The Supreme Court and the Commander in Chief* (Ithaca: Cornell University Press, 1951), 17.

56. 343 U.S. 579 (1952).

57. 418 U.S. 683 (1974).

58. Maeva Marcus, *Truman and the Steel Seizure Case: The Limits of Presidential Power* (New York: Columbia University Press, 1977).

59. Edward S. Corwin, "The Steel Seizure Case: A Judicial Brick Without Straw," *Columbia Law Review* 53 (1953): 53.

60. Harry S. Truman, *II Memoirs: Years of Trial and Hope* (Garden City, N.Y.: Doubleday, 1956), 475–78.

61. 418 U.S. 683 (1974). Choper, *Judicial Review*, 306.

62. *Nixon* v. *Fitzgerald*, 457 U.S. 731 (1982).

63. *Goldwater* v. *Carter*, 444 U.S. 996 (1979).

64. *Dames & Moore* v. *Regan*, 453 U.S. 654 (1981).

65. *Haig* v. *Agee*, 453 U.S. 280 (1981); *Regan* v. *Wald*, 468 U.S. 222 (1984).

66. *United States* v. *Stanley*, 107 S. Ct. 3054 (1987); *Solario* v. *United States*, 107 S. Ct. 2924 (1987).

67. Reagan quoted, *New York Times*, 16 May 1987, p. 1. See *ibid.*, 19 May 1987, p. A34.

68. *Wall Street Journal*, 5 May 1987, p. 36.

69. *Carter* v. *Carter Coal Co.*, 298 U.S. 238, 328 (1936).

70. *United States* v. *United States District Court*, 407 U.S. 247 (1972).

71. Alexander Bickel, "Forward: The Passive Virtues," *Harvard Law Review* 75 (1961): 64.

72. Clinton Rossiter, *The American Presidency*, 2d ed. (New York: Harcourt, Brace, 1960), 58.

73. 395 U.S. 486 (1986).

74. *Gravel* v. *United States*, 408 U.S. 606 (1972).

75. *Hutchinson* v. *Proxmire*, 443 U.S. 111 (1979).

76. *Panama Refining Co.* v. *Ryan*, 293 U.S. 388 (1935); *Schechter Poultry Co.* v. *United States*, 295 U.S. 495, 553 (1935).

77. Jackson, J., in *FTC* v. *Ruberoid Co.*, 343 U.S. 470, 487 (1952).

78. Francis E. Rourke, "Bureaucracy in the American Constitutional Order," *Political Science Quarterly* 102 (1987): 217.

79. 462 U.S. 919 (1983).

80. *Ibid.*, p. 959.

81. Louis Fisher, "Judicial Misjudgments about the Lawmaking Process: the Legislative Veto Cases," *Public Administration Review* 45 (November, 1985): 705. See *New York Times*, 17 May 1986, p. 7; and 21 January 1987, p. A25.

82. Not for attribution.

83. *U.S. Constitution*, Art. II, sec. 2.

84. 424 U.S. 1 (1976).

85. 106 S. Ct. 3181 (1986).

86. White, J., *ibid.*, p. 3205; *New York Times*, 8 July 1986, p. 3205.

87. *Myers* v. *United States*, 272 U.S. 524 (1926); *Humphrey's Executor* v. *United States*, 295 U.S. 602 (1934).
88. *New York Times*, 1 March 1986, p. 32.
89. *New York Times*, 6 November 1985, p. B8.
90. *Synar* v. *United States*, 626 F. Supp. 1374 (D.D.C. 1986).
91. *New York Times*, 27 April 1986, p. E5.
92. *American Textile Mfrs.* v. *Donovan*, 452 U.S. 490 (1981); quote, Antonin Scalia, "A Note on the Benzene Case," *Regulation* (July-August, 1980), as quoted in *National Law Journal*, 30 June 1986, p. 20.
93. *Ticor Title Insurance* v. *FTC*, No. 86-5078; see *National Law Journal*, 13 October 1986, p. 23.
94. *New York Times*, 25 June 1986, p. B6.
95. *Barnes* v. *Kline*, 759 F. 2d 21 (D.C. Cir. 1985); mooted in *Burke* v. *Barnes*, 107 S. Ct. 734 (1987). See *New York Times*, 26 February 1988, p. B9.
96. *New York Times*, 23 February 1988, p. D29, and 23 January 1988, pp. A1 and quote, A8. *Morrison* v. *Olson*, 818 F. 2d 34 (D.C. Cir. Indep. Coun. Div. 1987), and No. 87-1279.
97. *Ex parte Siebold*, 100 U.S. 371 (1879); *New York Times*, 11 July 1987, p. A8. Cf. the views of Anthony Lewis, _New York Times, 4 March 1987, p. A 27, and Assistant Attorney General John R. Bolton, *ibid.*, 11 June 1987, p. A1. For other independent counsel cases, see, e.g., *In re Sealed Case*, No. 87-5186 and *North* v. *Walsh*, Nos. 87-869 and 87-1094; and *Deaver* v. *Seymour*, No. 87-0477.
98. Robert H. Jackson to Frank Murphy, 16 February 1942, Frank Murphy Papers, Michigan Historical Collections, University of Michigan.
99. Choper, *Judicial Review*, 260-415.
100. Willard Hurst, "Review and the Distribution of National Powers," in Edmond Cahn, ed., *Supreme Court and Supreme Law* (Bloomington, Ind.: Indiana University Press, 1954), 158-69.
101. Gerald Gunther, *Constitutional Law*, 11th ed. (Mineola, N.Y.: Foundation Press, 1985), 337.

Index